The Words Worth Eating

Healthy Heart Cookbook

Delicious Low-Fat, Low-Cholesterol Recipes
with Diabetic Exchanges

by Jacquelyn G. Legg

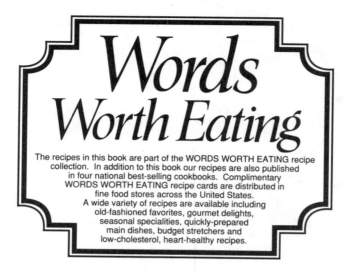

Words Worth Eating

The recipes in this book are part of the WORDS WORTH EATING recipe
collection. In addition to this book our recipes are also published
in four national best-selling cookbooks. Complimentary
WORDS WORTH EATING recipe cards are distributed in
fine food stores across the United States.
A wide variety of recipes are available including
old-fashioned favorites, gourmet delights,
seasonal specialities, quickly-prepared
main dishes, budget stretchers and
low-cholesterol, heart-healthy recipes.

WORDS WORTH EATING COOKBOOKS:

• THE WORDS WORTH EATING COOKBOOK (12.95)

• THE WORDS WORTH EATING
LOW CHOLESTEROL COOKBOOK - BOOK ONE (3.95)

• THE WORDS WORTH EATING
LOW CHOLESTEROL COOKBOOK - BOOK TWO (3.95)

• THE WORDS WORTH EATING
SEAFOOD COOKBOOK (3.95)

• THE WORDS WORTH EATING
HEALTHY HEART COOKBOOK (4.95)

For copies of any of the above books send price of book plus $3.00
postage and handling to:
WORDS WORTH EATING, 10 Milford Road, Newport News, VA 23601
Make checks payable to WORDS WORTH EATING.
Virginia residents add 4½% sales tax.

Words Worth Eating Healthy Heart Cookbook
Copyright 1991

Printings:
March, 1991; July, 1991; July, 1992

ISBN 0-924713-46-1

Nutritional analysis provided by Jeanine M. Sherry, M.S., R.D. (Registered Dietitian/
Nutrition Consultant). The computerized nutritional analysis has been rounded to
the nearest tenth or the nearest whole number, as appropriate.

Suggested retail price: $4.95

Who Needs A Healthy Heart Cookbook?
Everybody . . .

Dear Healthy Cook,

Good food and good living go hand in hand. A lifestyle which embraces the philosophy of fitness, fun and good food is the key to good health. Today's move towards better living, in spite of demanding schedules, calls for nutritious, well-balanced meals which can be made in a hurry.

Recent reports by the prestigious National Academy of Sciences, the National Cholesterol Education Program, the American Heart Association and the American Cancer Society state that the total amount and type of fat in your diet can influence your risk of obesity and cancer — not just heart disease.

Health experts around the world are recommending a diet rich in whole grains, vegetables and fruits, while sparing in fat and sodium, to help prevent or treat all of the following chronic disease conditions:

- Heart Disease
- Cancer
- Obesity
- High Blood Pressure
- Diabetes

Nutrition-minded cooks, whether interested in shedding a few pounds, treating a specific disease condition or in just maintaining good health, will welcome THE WORDS WORTH EATING HEALTHY HEART COOKBOOK. Over 65 exciting new recipes are included, all with nutritional information and diabetic exchanges.

Recipes are quick and easy to prepare and are trimmed of unwanted fat and cholesterol. The use of herbs and spices and limited salt enhances the natural flavor and color of vegetables, meat, poultry and fresh fish.

"Kiss the butter and oil goodbye and welcome the delicious flavor of healthy eating the whole family will love."

Jacquelyn G. Legg
Author

Jeanine M. Sherry
Registered Dietitian/Nutrition Consultant

Children, Teenagers and Pregnant or Breast-Feeding Women . . .
should consult their family doctor or nutritionist before modifying their diet.

TABLE OF CONTENTS

TABLE OF CONTENTS

> To assist you in following a low-fat diet, all recipes in this cookbook meet the following criteria:
> • 30% or less of total calories from fat
> or
> • 3 grams or less of fat per serving
> The goal for a low-fat diet is to balance fat intake over the entire day, rather than for each meal or food item.

HEALTHY HEART "LIFE-SAVERS"

These recipes will be "life-savers" in the kitchen by allowing you to recreate the same wonderful recipes you've always loved—and they're "life-savers" because they will allow you to reduce fat and cholesterol in your daily diet.

NO CHOLESTEROL EGG SUBSTITUTE*
"Equals 2 whole eggs!"

3 egg whites
1 teaspoon vegetable oil (safflower oil
  or canola oil is recommended)

1 tablespoon non-fat dry milk solids
dash salt
food coloring

Blend ingredients together and use in recipes calling for whole eggs. This is a delicious alternative for those on cholesterol restricted diets. It contains no cholesterol, reduced fat and calories and more protein than 2 whole eggs.

Note: Experiment to find a color that appeals to you. Try 1 drop of yellow and 2 specks of red (put a tiny bit ot food coloring on the tine of a fork for a speck — then swish in egg mixture). The no cholesterol egg substitute recipe works well in baked products where whole eggs are called for. It makes great scrambled eggs, can be used in baked custards, quiches and similar dishes. With this recipe, you will experience a lighter, fluffier egg. The substitute is not appropriate for recipes using large quantities of egg yolks needed for thickening.

Recipe provided by the Virginia Egg Council, Harrisonburg, Virginia 22801.

Nutritional Analysis Per 1 Egg Equivalent

Calories: 52	Protein: 6 g	Saturated Fat: 0.2 g
Cholesterol: 0 mg	Carbohydrate: 2 g	Polyunsaturated Fat: 0.6 g
Sodium: 209 mg	Total Fat: 2.3 g	Monounsaturated Fat: 1.5 g

Diabetic Exchange: 1 lean meat

HOMEMADE "SOUR CREAM"*
"Low in cholesterol and fat!"

1 1/2 cups 1% cream-style cottage
  cheese
1–2 teaspoons fresh lemon juice

1–2 tablespoons buttermilk or skim
milk (optional, depending on desired
consistency)

Place all ingredients in food processor and process, using steel blade, until thick and completely smooth. Store in an airtight container; keep chilled until ready to use. Yields 1 1/2 cups.

SERVING SUGGESTIONS: The uses for this no-fat "sour cream" are many. With a little experimentation you will find your own favorite ones. Here are a few from WORDS WORTH EATING:

* add chopped chives and green onions and use as a topping for baked potatoes
* add Dijon mustard and lemon zest and spoon over hot, steamed vegetables
* add additional buttermilk or skim milk, a small amount of corn oil, lemon pepper and garlic powder or garlic salt and serve over a green salad
* use to replace sour cream in your favorite recipes
* use to replace cream in cold, cream-based soups

Nutritional Analysis Per Tablespoon

Calories: 10	Protein: 2 g	Saturated Fat: 0 g
Cholesterol: 1 mg	Carbohydrate: 1 g	Polyunsaturated Fat: 0 g
Sodium: 54 mg	Total Fat: 0 g	Monounsaturated Fat: 0 g

Diabetic Exchange: 1–2 tablespons = free food

HEALTHY HEART "LIFE-SAVERS"

UNBELIEVABLE WHITE SAUCE*
"Contains no fat!"

This sauce can be used in all recipes calling for white sauce.
The seasonings can be varied to your personal taste.

1 1/2 cups skim milk
3 tablespoons cream of rice cereal

1/8 teaspoon dry mustard
1/8 teaspoon salt (optional)

Place milk in a small saucepan which has a tight-fitting lid; heat uncovered until milk comes to a boil. Stir in cereal and seasonings; cook uncovered for 1 minute, stirring contstantly. Remove from heat, cover and let stand 5 minutes. Place thickened cereal in food processor and process, using steel blade, until completely smooth. Yields approximately 2 cups.

Note: Sauce can be prepared a day ahead and kept in refrigerator until ready to use. Heat sauce in microwave; add additional ingredients just before serving.

"This white sauce will allow you to recreate sauces that you thought you'd never be able to eat again!"

Nutritional Analysis Per Tablespoon without Salt

Calories: 16	Protein: 1 g	Saturated Fat: 0
Cholesterol: 0.6 mg	Carbohydrate: 3 g	Polyunsaturated Fat: 0
Sodium: 18 mg	Total Fat: 0	Monounsaturated Fat: 0

Diabetic Exchange: 1 tablespoon = free food

 **"LIFE-SAVER" SAUCES***
"Made with Unbelievable White Sauce!"

- *CHEESE SAUCE — Add 2-3 ounces low-fat processed cheese and 1 teaspoon fresh lemon juice to hot white sauce; stir to melt. Serve on macaroni or vegetables.*
- *MORNAY SAUCE — Add 2-3 ounces grated low-fat Swiss Cheese and 1 teaspoon fresh lemon juice to hot white sauce; stir to melt. Serve on fresh asparagus or broiled chicken.*
- *LEMON MUSTARD SAUCE — Add 1-2 teaspoons fresh lemon juice, 1/4 teaspoon grated lemon rind and 1/4 teaspoon Dijon mustard to hot white sauce; stir to blend. Serve on seafood or vegetables.*
- *ALFREDO SAUCE — Season white sauce with 1/8–1/4 teaspoon garlic powder and a pinch nutmeg; pour over 1 pound of hot, cooked and drained fettucini and toss. Quickly stir in 1/4 cup freshly grated Parmesan cheese. Sprinkle with freshly chopped parsley and cracked pepper. Serve immediately to family and guests who'll never believe it's a low-fat dish! (If Alfredo Sauce gets too thick when cheese is added, stir in hot skim milk until sauce reaches desired consistency.)*
- *MUSHROOM SAUCE — Add 1 teaspoon white wine vinegar and 1 cup sliced, cooked mushrooms to hot white sauce. Mix with hot green beans; season with cracked black pepper.*

"Be creative; use this basic white sauce to recreate other favorite sauces, soups and entrées!"

HEALTHY HEART

SUMMERTIME MINT TEA
"Serve on hot afternoons!"

4 tea bags
12–16 large mint leaves
3 cups boiling water
1 cup sugar
1/4 cup fresh lemon juice
1 cup orange juice

1 1/2 quarts cold water
GARNISH:
12 sprigs of mint
1 orange, sliced
1 lemon, sliced

Place tea bags and mint leaves in a large heat-proof pitcher; add boiling water and allow to steep for 10 minutes. Add sugar and stir very gently. Cool completely; stir and strain mixture. Discard tea bags and mint. Pour mixture back in pitcher; add all remaining ingredients except garnish. Serve over ice in tall glasses. Garnish with mint and fruit. Serves 8.

NOTE: Mint tea is a summer drink from our grandmother's day that soft drinks have yet to equal.

"Serve after golf or tennis!"

Nutritional Analysis Per Serving without Garnish

Calories: 105	Protein: 0	Saturated Fat: 0
Cholesterol: 0	Carbohydrate: 28 g	Polyunsaturated Fat: 0
Sodium: 10 mg	Total Fat: 0	Monounsaturated Fat: 0

Diabetic Exchange: Substitute artificial sweetener for sugar and count as 1/2 fruit.

ORANGE JUICE SPARKLER
"Especially refreshing!"

1 1/2 cups orange juice
1/2 cup quinine or tonic water

2 slices orange, for garnish

Fill a tall glass with ice; pour in 3/4 cup orange juice. Top with 1/4 cup quinine or tonic water. Stir to mix. Garnish with an orange slice. Serves 2.

"Great on a hot summer day!"

Nutritional Analysis Per Serving

Calories: 102	Protein: 1 g	Saturated Fat: 0
Cholesterol: 0	Carbohydrate: 25 g	Polyunsaturated Fat: 0
Sodium: 7 mg	Total Fat:0	Monounsaturated Fat: 0

Diabetic Exchange: Substitute diet tonic water and count as 1 1/2 fruits.

GOLDEN WEDDING PUNCH
"Served over lemon sherbet!"

2 cups sugar
1 1/2 cups fresh mint leaves
2 cups boiling water
3/4 cup frozen lemon juice
1 12-ounce can apricot nectar
1 6-ounce can frozen limeade
  concentrate, thawed
1 6-ounce can frozen orange juice
  concentrate, thawed

1 12-ounce can unsweetened
  pineapple juice
2 1-liter bottles club soda, chilled
1 quart lemon sherbet
GARNISH:
1 lemon, sliced
1 orange, sliced
3–4 sprigs fresh mint
6–8 strawberries

Place sugar, mint leaves and boiling water in a heat-proof pitcher; stir to dissolve sugar. Cool to room temperature; strain and chill. Mix strained mixture with all remaining ingredients except club soda, sherbet and garnish. Chill overnight or as long as 2–3 days. When ready to serve, pour into punch bowl; add club soda. Float scoops of lemon sherbet in bowl. Garnish with slices of lemon, orange, fresh mint and strawberries. Yields 24 servings.

"Use for weddings, showers and anniversaries!"

Nutritional Analysis Per Serving

Calories: 147	Protein: 1 g	Saturated Fat: 0
Cholesterol: 2 mg	Carbohydrate: 36 g	Polyunsaturated Fat: 0
Sodium: 34 mg	Total Fat: 0	Monounsaturated Fat: 0
	(Not appropriate for diabetics)	

CRANBERRY PUNCH
"Wonderful ruby color!"

1 cup fresh orange juice
1/2 cup fresh lemon juice
16 ounces cranberry juice cocktail
1–1 1/4 cups sugar

3–4 cups chilled soda water
1 orange, sliced, for garnish
1 lemon, sliced, for garnish

Combine first 4 ingredients; stir to dissolve sugar. Add soda water and pour over ice in a large pitcher. Yields 1/2 gallon or 16 4-ounce servings. Garnish with orange and lemon slices.

NOTE: Larger quantities can be served over ice in a punch bowl. If punch is not to be served immediately, reduce amount of water and increase amount of ice.

"Beautiful color and delicious taste!"

Nutritional Analysis Per Serving without Garnish

Calories: 72	Protein: 0	Saturated Fat: 0
Cholesterol: 0	Carbohydrate: 19 g	Polyunsaturated Fat: 0
Sodium: 2 mg	Total Fat: 0	Monounsaturated Fat: 0

Diabetic Exchange: Substitute artificial sweetener for sugar and count as 1/2 fruit

MELON BALLS WITH FRESH LIME DRESSING
"Serve as appetizer, salad or dessert!"

MELON BALLS:
1 cup honeydew balls
1 cup cantaloupe balls
1 cup watermelon balls
or
3 cups of all one kind of melon balls

LIME DRESSING:
1 cup water
2 tablespoons sugar
2 tablespoons fresh lime juice
GARNISH:
5–6 sprigs fresh mint
1 lime, sliced

Prepare melon balls, cover with plastic wrap and chill.
DRESSING: Combine water and sugar in small saucepan; bring to boil. Boil for 2 minutes; remove from heat and add lime juice. Allow dressing to cool to room temperature; pour over melon balls. Chill in dressing for several hours before serving. When ready to serve, pour undrained melon balls into shallow glass dish. Garnish with mint and sliced lime. Yields 6 half-cup servings.

NOTE: Also delicious with fresh pineapple cubes, sliced bananas or apple slices.

"For a great dessert, spoon melon and dressing over low-fat frozen yogurt or sherbet!"

Nutritional Analysis Per Serving

Calories: 44	Protein: 1 g	Saturated Fat: 0
Cholesterol: 0	Carbohydrate: 11 g	Polyunsaturated Fat: 0
Sodium: 6 mg	Total Fat:0	Monounsaturated Fat: 0

Diabetic Exchange: 3/4 fruit

MARINATED VEGETABLE PLATTER
"Crisp and flavorful"

1 cup fresh button mushroom caps
1 cup cauliflower flowerets
1 cup carrots, sliced diagonally
1 cup yellow squash, sliced diagonally
1 cup zucchini, sliced diagonally
1 cup cherry tomatoes
1 bunch green onions
MARINADE:
1/4 cup white wine vinegar

4 tablespoons frozen apple juice
  concentrate
1 shallot, minced
1 clove garlic, minced
1 1/2–2 teaspoons Dijon mustard
1/8 teaspoon hot pepper sauce
1–2 teaspoons fresh lemon juice
4 tablespoons extra-virgin olive oil
1/4 teaspoon freshly ground black pepper

Individually steam the first 5 vegetables until just tender. DO NOT OVERCOOK! Plunge vegetables into a large pan of ice water to stop cooking and to preserve color. Drain well and dry vegetables on toweling. Place in a large plastic bag. Mix together marinade ingredients and pour over vegetables in bag; close tightly.

Recipe continues on page 9.

Marinate overnight; turn bag often. When ready to serve, place drained vegetables on a flat platter. Garnish with cherry tomatoes and whole green onions. Serves 24 as an appetizer or 12 as a salad.

"Also serve as a salad for cookouts and buffet dinners!"

Nutritional Analysis Per Serving as an Appetizer (as a Salad)
Calories: 20 (40) Protein: 0 (1) g Saturated Fat: 0.2 (0.4) g
Cholesterol: 0 (0) Carbohydrate: 2 (5) g Polyunsaturated Fat: 0.1 (0.2) g
Sodium: 6 (13) mg Total Fat: 1.2 (2.4) g Monounsaturated Fat: 0.9 (1.8) g
Note: A portion of food containing 3 grams or less of fat is considered a low-fat serving.
Diabetic Exchanges as an Appetizer: 1/2 vegetable, 1/4 fat

GRILLED FAJITAS WITH CHERRY TOMATO SALSA
"Cooked on the grill for added flavor!"

1 pound flank steak
8 small soft flour tortillas
3 tablespoons light sour cream
3 green onions, chopped
MARINADE:
1/4 cup canola oil
1 tablespoon fresh lemon juice
1 tablespoon teriyaki sauce
1 tablespoon prepared mustard
1 tablespoon Worcestershire sauce
1 tablespoon chopped onion
1 clove garlic, minced
1 jalapeño pepper, sliced and seeded

1 slice lemon
1/2 teaspoon cracked black pepper
CHERRY TOMATO SALSA:
1 pint cherry tomatoes, quartered
1/4 teaspoon salt
1/2 cup chopped red onion
1/2 cup sweet yellow pepper
1-2 jalapeño peppers, diced
2 tablespoons fresh cilantro or parsley, minced
1 lime, juiced
1/4 teaspoon black pepper

MARINADE: Combine all marinade ingredients; set aside.

SALSA: Combine salsa ingredients; let stand at room temperature for 2–3 hours.

FLANK STEAK; Remove all excess fat. Pound meat with a mallet or cleaver to tenderize. Marinate overnight. To grill; drain and cook over a hot fire 5–6 minutes per side. Do not overcook. Slice in extra-thin diagonal slices; reserve meat juices.

TO HEAT TORTILLAS: Place on a microwave-safe dish, cover with plastic wrap and heat at 80% power, just long enough to warm tortillas.

TO SERVE: While tortillas heat, mound sliced meat in the center of a platter; top with reserved meat juices. Serve with tortillas, salsa, sour cream and green onions. Allow each person to fill and roll their own. As an appetizer, cut tortilla in half before filling; yields 16 halves. As an entrée, leave whole; yields 8. Serves 16 as an appetizer or 4 as an entrée.

Note: Boneless chicken breasts are also delicious in this recipe.

"Fajitas, often called Mexican steak sandwiches, are a Tex-Mex specialty!"

Nutritional Analysis Per Filled Tortilla Half (Per Filled Whole Tortilla) with Salsa and Toppings
Calories: 106 (212) Protein: 8 (17) g Saturated Fat: 1.0 (2.0) g
Cholesterol: 17 (35) mg Carbohydrate: 11 (21) g Polyunsaturated Fat: 0.7 (1.3) g
Sodium: 73 (145) mg Total Fat: 3.4 (6.8) g Monounsaturated Fat: 1.7 (3.5) g
% of calories from fat = 29 (29)%
Diabetic Exchanges: 1 lean meat, 1/2 bread, 1 vegetable (1 1/2 lean meats, 1 bread, 1 vegetable, 1/2 fat)

HEALTHY HEART

FRESH FRUIT SALAD
"Topped with a delicious yogurt dressing!"

8 leaves romaine lettuce, shredded
1/2 cup fresh pineapple, cut into
   1-inch cubes
1/2 cup melon, cut into 1-inch cubes
1 orange, peeled and diced
1 apple, unpared and sliced
1/2 cup seedless white grapes
12 strawberries, washed, hulled
   and sliced

YOGURT DRESSING:
1/4 cup vanilla non-fat yogurt
   or
1/4 cup plain non-fat yogurt
1 tablespoon orange juice
2 tablespoons finely diced fresh
   pineapple
pinch nutmeg
pinch ground cinnamon
6–8 sprigs fresh mint, for garnish

Place lettuce on flat serving dish; arrange prepared fruit on top of lettuce. Cover and refrigerate. Mix yogurt with remaining dressing ingredients and stir. When ready to serve, drizzle dressing on top of fruit dish; garnish with mint. Serves 8.

"Spectacular looking and great tasting!"

Nutritional Analysis Per Serving with Dressing

Calories 44:	Protein: 1 g	Saturated Fat: 0
Cholesterol: 0	Carbohydrate: 10 g	Polyunsaturated Fat: 0
Sodium: 9 mg	Total Fat: 0	Monounsaturated Fat: 0

Diabetic Exchange: 3/4 fruit, using plain non-fat yogurt or artificially sweetened vanilla yogurt

MOLDED COLE SLAW
"Great with seafood or barbecue!"

2 envelopes unflavored gelatin
1/2 cup cold water
2 cups boiling water
1/2 cup sugar
1/2 cup vinegar
2 tablespoons lemon juice
1/2 teaspoon salt

1 cup cabbage, shredded finely
2 cups chopped celery
1/4 cup chopped pimento
2 tablespoons chopped green pepper
2 tablespoons chopped parsley
2 tablespoons chopped pimento-stuffed
   olives

Soften gelatin in cold water. Add sugar, vinegar, lemon juice and salt to boiling water. Add gelatin to heated mixture and stir until gelatin is completely dissolved. Add remaining ingredients, mix well and pour into salad mold or glass bowl. Chill until firm. Serves 10.

NOTE: This wonderful, tart cole slaw can be made 1 or 2 days ahead. Serve with The "Ultimate" Barbecue on page 36. It is also delicious with baked, broiled or grilled seafood and spoonbread.

"You'll be making this again!"

Nutritional Analysis Per Serving

Calories: 54	Protein: 2 g	Saturated Fat: 0
Cholesterol: 0	Carbohydrate: 12 g	Polyunsaturated Fat: 0
Sodium: 138 g	Total Fat: 0	Monounsaturated Fat: 0

Diabetic Exchange: Substitute artificial sweetener for sugar and count as 1 vegetable.

TOMATO ASPIC WITH SHRIMP
"The perfect luncheon salad!"

1 tablespoon unflavored gelatin
2 teaspoons sugar
14 ounces V-8 juice
1/2 teaspoon Worcestershire sauce
2 tablespoons fresh lemon juice
1/3 cup celery, diced

2 tablespoons pimento-stuffed olives, sliced
4 teaspoons sour cream dressing (see below)
4 lettuce leaves
16 medium shrimp, steamed and cleaned

Mix gelatin and sugar in small saucepan. Slowly add half of V-8 juice, stirring well. Cook over medium heat, stirring constantly, until gelatin dissolves. Remove from heat and stir in rest of V-8 juice, Worcestershire, lemon juice, celery and olives. Fill 4 custard cups or small salad molds and chill until firm. Make Sour Cream Dressing and chill. To serve, remove aspic from cups or molds and place on lettuce. Surround each salad with 4 shrimp and top salad with Sour Cream Dressing (see below). Serves 4.

"A spicy salad accompaniment for all seafood dishes!"

Nutritional Analysis Per Serving of Aspic and Shrimp without Dressing

Calories: 85	Protein: 7 g	Saturated Fat: 10.2 g
Cholesterol: 37 mg	Carbohydrate: 11 g	Polyunsaturated Fat: 0.8 g
Sodium: 435 mg	Total Fat: 1.3 g	Monounsaturated Fat: 0.3 g
	% of calories from fat = 11%	

Diabetic Exchanges: 2 vegetables, 1/2 lean meat

SOUR CREAM DRESSING
"A dressing with a zip!"

1 cup light sour cream or homemade sour cream (see page 4)
1/2 cup reduced-calorie mayonnaise
2 teaspoons lemon juice
1 teaspoon prepared horseradish

1/8 teaspoon of cayenne pepper
1/4 teaspoon salt
1/8 teaspoon paprika
1/4 teaspoon dry mustard

Combine all ingredients and mix thoroughly. Chill until ready to serve.

Nutritional Analysis Per Tablespoon of Dressing

Calories: 25	Protein: 0	Saturated Fat: 0.2 g
Cholesterol: 4 mg	Carbohydrate: 1 g	Polyunsaturated Fat: 1.5 g
Sodium: 28 mg	Total Fat: 2.0 g	Monounsaturated Fat: 0.3 g

Note: A portion of food containing 3 grams or less of fat is considered a low-fat serving.
Diabetic Exchanges: 1 teaspoon — 1 tablespoon = free food

 SERVING SUGGESTION FOR SOUR CREAM DRESSING
The Sour Cream Dressing is delicious to serve on seafood salads, broiled fish steaks and cold sliced roast beef.

CURRIED CHICKEN SALAD WITH ALMONDS
"With a creamy dressing that tastes too rich to be legal!"

4 cups cooked boneless, skinless
   chicken breasts, cut in bite-size pieces
1/4 cup sliced almonds, toasted
1/3 cup raisins
DRESSING
1/3 cup fat-free sour cream
1/3 cup reduced-calorie mayonnaise
1/3 cup vanilla fat-free yogurt
1 tablespoon finely diced chutney
1 teaspoon fresh lemon juice

1 teaspoon diced red onion
1/4 teaspoon curry powder, or more, to
   taste
GARNISH:
8 leaves lettuce
16 cantaloupe or honeydew slices
4 cups fresh strawberries
8 bunches white grapes
1/4 cup sliced almonds, toasted

Place chicken, almonds and raisins in a large bowl. Prepare dressing by mixing all dressing ingredients together in a medium bowl; pour over chicken. Stir to coat chicken and allow to chill for 4-6 hours or overnight

TO SERVE: Spoon chicken salad onto a decorative lettuce leaf and surround with seasonal melon, strawberries and grape clusters; sprinkle with toasted almonds. Serves 8.

NOTE: The amount of curry called for is very mild; curry lovers may wish to increase the amount.

AS AN APPETIZER SPREAD: Finely mince chicken, raisins and nuts; mix with rest of ingredients. Chill. Use as a spread on low-fat wheat crackers.

"Serve with fresh asparagus or steamed broccoli and Popover Muffins (page 20). Sensational!"

Nutritional Analysis Per Serving with Garnish

Calories: 256	Protein: 18 g	Saturated Fat: 1.0 g
Cholesterol: 40 mg	Carbohydrate: 30 g	Polyunsaturated Fat: 2.3 g
Sodium: 55 mg	Total Fat: 7.8 g	Monounsaturated Fat: 4.5 g

% of calories from fat = 27%
Diabetic Exchanges: 2 lean meats, 2 fruits

OTHER SALAD SUGGESTIONS
- *Melon Balls with Fresh Lime Dressing — page 8*
- *Marinated Vegetable Platter — page 8*
- *Winter Ambrosia — page 40*

MARINATED STEAK SALAD
"A meal in itself!"

1 12–14 ounce extra-lean sirloin or strip
  steak, approximately 1-inch thick
MARINADE:
1/2 cup reduced-sodium soy sauce
5 tablespoons sugar
1 tablespoon finely diced fresh ginger
2 cloves garlic, minced
SALAD GREENS:
8 cups leaf lettuce washed, dried
  and torn into bite-size pieces
1 cup sliced cucumber
1 cup sliced red onion

SALAD DRESSING:
1/4 cup reduced-sodium soy sauce
2 tablespoons fresh lemon juice
3/4 teaspoon minced fresh jalapeño
  pepper
2 tablespoons peanut oil
2 tablespoons extra-virgin olive oil
GARNISH:
8 cherry tomatoes
1/2 cup sliced sweet yellow pepper
1/4 cup fresh cilantro or parsley, minced

Trim steak of all fat; set aside. Prepare marinade and pour over steak; cover and allow to marinate several hours at room temperature. Prepare salad ingredients and chill. Combine all dressing ingredients; whisk to blend and set aside. When ready to serve: grill steak over a hot fire 3–5 minutes per side. DO NOT OVERCOOK! Remove from grill and let stand for 5–10 minutes before slicing in extra-thin slices. While meat is being prepared, place greens on individual plates; top each with 1–2 teaspoons of dressing. Place approximately 3 ounces steak on each salad; garnish with cherry tomatoes, pepper and cilantro or parsley. Serves 4.

SERVING SUGGESTION: Top with freshly cracked black pepper and serve with crusty bread.

NOTE: The marinade is also excellent on chicken or seafood. The salad dressing can be used on Oriental green salads and as a delicious sauce for grilled fish steaks.

"A real show stopper with plenty of taste!

Nutritional Analysis Per Serving of Salad without Dressing

Calories: 231	Protein: 27 g	Saturated Fat: 1.7 g
Cholesterol: 57 mg	Carbohydrate: 20 g	Polyunsaturated Fat: 1.0 g
Sodium: 662 mg	Total Fat: 5.7 g	Monounsaturated Fat: 3.0 g

% of calories from fat = 22%
Diabetic Exchanges: 2 1/2 lean meats, 1 bread and 1 vegetable

Nutritional Analysis Per Teaspoon of Dressing

Calories: 18	Protein: 0	Saturated Fat: 0.3 g
Cholesterol: 0 mg	Carbohydrate: 0	Polyunsaturated Fat: 0.4 g
Sodium: 80 mg	Total Fat: 1.8 g	Monounsaturated Fat: 1.1 g

Note: A portion of food containing 3 grams or less of fat is considered a low-fat serving.
Diabetic Exchanges: 1 teaspoon = free; 1 tablespoon = 1 fat

SUMMERTIME CHICKEN AND FRESH CORN CHOWDER
"The better the corn, the better the chowder!"

1 2 1/2–3 pound chicken, cut up
   with skin removed (yields
   approximately 4 cups cooked chicken)
1 quart water
3 ribs celery with leaves
2 sprigs parsley
1 cup chopped onion
1 bay leaf
10 whole peppercorns
2 10 3/4-ounce cans low-sodium chicken
   broth, defatted

1 teaspoon instant chicken bouillon
   granules
3 cups diced cooked potatoes
3 cups diced cooked carrots
4 cups fresh corn kernels
   (approximately 8 ears corn)
8-10 ounces low-sodium chicken broth,
   defatted (optional)
GARNISH:
1/2 cup light sour cream or plain non-fat
   yogurt
4 tablespoons fresh minced parsley

Put chicken, water and next 5 ingredients in a large covered pot; bring to boil, reduce heat to low and cook for 1–1 1/2 hours or until chicken is tender. Remove chicken pieces from broth; cool chicken. Strain broth and chill to allow fat to harden; discard fat. Return strained broth to pot; cut chicken in bite-size chunks and add to strained broth. Add 2 cans of broth, bouillon granules, potatoes and carrots; cook on medium-low heat for 30–40 minutes. Remove from heat and stir in corn and additional broth, if desired, to make a thinner soup; return to heat and cook gently over low heat for 5–10 minutes or until corn is tender. DO NOT BOIL! Spoon chowder into bowls; top with 1 1/2 teaspoons sour cream or yogurt and a generous sprinkling of parsley. Yields 6 12-ounce servings.

NOTE: To defat cooked or canned chicken broth, chill broth overnight to allow fat to harden.

WINTERTIME NOTE: When corn is not at its peak flavor, use small-kernel fresh or frozen corn; follow all cooking and serving directions. Top each bowl with 1 tablespoon tomato salsa and serve with light tortilla chips for a chicken and corn chowder with a Southwest taste!

"Serve with a large tossed salad and crusty French bread for a hearty, healthy dinner!"

Nutritional Analysis Per 12-Ounce Serving without Garnish

Calories: 373	Protein: 34 g	Saturated Fat: 1.9 g
Cholesterol: 78 mg	Carbohydrate: 50 g	Polyunsaturated Fat: 2.5 g
Sodium: 300 mg	Total Fat: 5.8 g	Monounsaturated Fat: 1.4 g

% of calories from fat = 14%
Diabetic Exchanges Per Cup: 2 lean meats, 2 breads

FARM WIFE'S TURKEY CHOWDER
"A delicious way to use a leftover turkey carcass!"

1 roasted turkey carcass, all skin
   removed
2 quarts low-sodium chicken broth,
   defatted
2 bay leaves
6–8 peppercorns
6–8 large sprigs parsley
2 cloves garlic, minced
2 cups diced potatoes
1 cup diced carrots
1 cup chopped onions

2 sprigs fresh marjoram
   or
1/8 teaspoon dried marjoram
2 leaves fresh sage
   or
1/8 teaspoon dried sage
1/4 teaspoon pepper
1/4 teaspoon dry mustard
1 cup diced cooked turkey
2 cups medium white sauce (see below)

Place turkey carcass in a large, heavy kettle; cover with 2 quarts chicken broth. Add bay leaves, peppercorns, parsley, and garlic. Bring to boil, reduce heat and cook covered over low heat for 1 1/2 hours. Strain broth and chill to remove all fat. Return broth to pot and add all remaining ingredients except white sauce. Cook until vegetables are tender. Add 1 1/2–2 cups white sauce to thicken to desired consistency. Serves 8.

WHITE SAUCE

2 tablespoons corn oil margarine
2 tablespoons flour
1/4 teaspoon dry mustard

1/8 teaspoon white pepper
2 cups evaporated skim milk

Melt margarine in a medium saucepan; stir in flour and allow to bubble for 2–3 minutes. Add dry mustard and white pepper; mix well. Remove from heat and add milk; stir with wire whisk until smooth. Return to heat and cook over low heat until thickened.

NOTE: *If the carcass has bits and pieces of dressing, all the better!*

"You'll never throw a turkey carcass out again!"

Nutritional Analysis Per 12-Ounce Serving

Calories: 237	Protein: 25 g	Saturated Fat: 2.0 g
Cholesterol: 40 mg	Carbohydrate: 19 g	Polyunsaturated Fat: 1.5 g
Sodium: 144 mg	Total Fat: 6.0 g	Monounsaturated Fat: 2.5 g

% of calories from fat = 24%

Diabetic Exchanges: 1 bread, 1 vegetable, 3 lean meats

♥SOUP AND SALAD
Serve a bowl of soup with a hot Popover Muffin (page 20) and Fresh Fruit Salad (page 10).

CRAB AND CHICKEN GUMBO
"A meal in itself!"

4 pounds chicken pieces, skin
  removed
4 cups water
1 cup celery pieces
1 cup chopped onions
2 cloves garlic, chopped
2 bay leaves
8 peppercorns
6 whole cloves
5 cups water
4 cups fresh ripe tomatoes, peeled and
  diced
1 cup sliced okra

1 medium green pepper, diced
1 medium sweet red pepper, diced
1/2 cup diced onion
1 cup fresh small-kernel corn
2 tablespoons Worcestershire sauce
1/4 teaspoon hot pepper sauce, or
  to taste
2 teaspoons filé powder
1/2 pound crab meat
6 cups cooked rice
GARNISH:
3 tomatoes, diced
1/2 cup chopped green onions

Place chicken and next 7 ingredients in a large covered pot; cook over medium heat until meat falls off the bones. Remove meat from broth and strain broth. Chill broth to remove all fat. Chop chicken into bite-size pieces. When fat has been removed from broth, return broth and chicken to large soup pot; add 5 additional cups of water and next 8 ingredients. Cook uncovered on low heat for 1 hour. Stir in filé powder and crab meat. Reheat gently; do not allow to boil after filé powder and crabmeat are added. Spoon 1/2 cup rice into each soup bowl, top with gumbo, diced tomatoes and green onions. Serves 12 generously.

Note: Gumbo is best when the vegetables are fresh! Filé powder is powdered sassafras and is essential for the authentic taste of gumbo.

"A New Orleans specialty!"

Nutritional Analysis Per Serving

Calories: 317	Protein: 29 g	Saturated Fat: 1.8 g
Cholesterol: 87 mg	Carbohydrate: 36 g	Polyunsaturated Fat: 1.5 g
Sodium: 178 mg	Total Fat: 5.8 g	Monounsaturated Fat: 2.5 g

% of calories from fat = 17%
Diabetic Exchanges: 2 breads, 1 vegetable, 3 lean meats

POTATO AND BACON CHOWDER
"Rich, hearty and extra low in fat!"

6 cups peeled and diced potatoes
1 quart skim milk
1 cup diced onion
1 cup diced celery, with leaves
2 chicken bouillion cubes
1/4 teaspoon dry mustard
1/4 teaspoon minced garlic

1/4 cup finely minced Canadian bacon
GARNISH:
8 teaspoons non-fat plain yogurt
2–3 teaspoons minced green onion tops
1–2 teaspoons freshly ground black
  pepper

Place first 7 ingredients in a large saucepan; bring to a boil and immediately reduce heat. Cover and cook over low heat until potatoes are very tender. Remove from heat and purée half of potato mixture in food processor; return mixture to pan and set aside. Sauté Canadian bacon in an ungreased teflon skillet until golden brown; add to chowder. Return chowder to heat and cook for 5 minutes. When ready to serve, ladle into bowls and top each serving with 1 teaspoon yogurt, a sprinkling of onions and a grinding of black pepper. Yields 6 12-ounce servings.

"Serve with thick slices of brown bread and a fresh fruit salad!"

Nutritional Analysis Per 12-Ounce Serving

Calories: 206	Protein: 11 g	Saturated Fat: 0.6 g
Cholesterol: 7 mg	Carbohydrate: 39 g	Polyunsaturated Fat: 0.2 g
Sodium: 522 mg	Total Fat: 1.3 g	Monounsaturated Fat: 0.5 g
	% of calories from fat = 5%	

Diabetic Exchanges: 1 skim milk, 1 1/2 breads

MEXICAN CHILI SALSA
"A South-of-the-Border soup sensation!"

1 pound extra-lean ground beef	1/8 teaspoon ground black pepper
1 medium onion, chopped	12 ounces unsalted tomato sauce
1 clove garlic, minced	1 quart water
1 16-ounce jar hot chunky salsa, divided	GARNISH:
1 26-ounce can kidney beans, undrained	8 teaspoons light sour cream
1 tablespoon chili powder	4 teaspoons chopped green onion
1/4 teaspoon dry mustard	tops

Brown beef, onion and garlic in an ungreased teflon frying pan; drain well on toweling. In a large saucepan combine beef mixture with 14 ounces salsa and remaining ingredients except garnish; bring to a boil. Cover and reduce heat to simmer; cook for 1 1/2 hours. Spoon into bowls and top each serving with 1 1/2 teaspoons remaining salsa, 1 teaspoon sour cream and a sprinkling of green onion. Yields 10 1-cup servings.

Note: This chili soup is not as thick as regular chili. This chili is also delicious when mixed with cooked brown rice.

"The salsa is the secret!"

Nutritional Analysis Per Serving
Note: First amount is per cup of chili with garnish; second amount is per 1/2 cup of chili with garnish and 1/2 cup cooked brown rice added.

Calories: 174 (192)	Protein: 17 (11) g	Saturated Fat: 1.8 (1.0) g
Cholesterol: 35 (17) mg	Carbohydrate: 22 (34) g	Polyunsaturated Fat: 1.3 (1.1) g
Sodium: 596 (299) mg	Total Fat: 4.1 (3.0) g	Monounsaturated Fat: 1.0 (0.9) g
	% of calories from fat = 19 (13) %	

Diabetic Exchanges: 1 bread, 1 1/2 lean meats, 1 vegetable (2 breads, 1/2 lean meat, 1 vegetable)

 SOUP AND CORNBREAD
Try a slice of toasted Double Cornbread with Cheddar (page 21) with a bowl of Mexican Chili Salsa.

HEALTHY HEART

PANCAKES WITH BLUEBERRY MAPLE SYRUP
"A breakfast treat!"

1 1/2 cups flour
1 teaspoon baking soda
1 teaspoon sugar
1 teaspoon grated orange rind
egg substitute equivalent to1 egg,
   lightly beaten

1 3/4 cups buttermilk
2 tablespoons tub margarine, melted
BLUEBERRY MAPLE SYRUP:
1/2 cup maple syrup
1/2 cup blueberries
1/8 teaspoon cinnamon

Sift first three ingredients; add orange rind and set aside. Mix egg substitute, buttermilk and margarine with a wire whisk until smooth. Make a well in the middle of the bowl of dry ingredients; add buttermilk mixture and stir until blended. DO NOT OVERMIX. Spoon batter onto a preheated, ungreased teflon-coated griddle; cook until bubbles appear in top surface. Turn and cook other side. Do not overcook! Yields 12 3–4 inch pancakes.

BLUEBERRY MAPLE SYRUP: During last few minutes of pancake cooking time, bring maple syrup to a boil. Add blueberries and poach for a few minutes. Spoon syrup over pancakes; sprinkle with cinnamon.

"The orange rind adds a special taste!"

Nutritional Analysis Per Pancake

Calories: 94	Protein: 3 g	Saturated Fat: 0.6 g
Cholesterol: 1 mg	Carbohydrate: 14 g	Polyunsaturated Fat: 1.0 g
Sodium: 140 mg	Total Fat: 2.5 g	Monounsaturated Fat: 0.9 g

% of calories from fat = 25%
Diabetic Exchanges: 1 bread, 1/2 fat

Nutritional Analysis Per Tablespoon of Syrup

Calories: 43	Protein: 0	Saturated Fat: 0
Cholesterol: 0 mg	Carbohydrate: 11 g	Polyunsaturated Fat: 0
Sodium: 24 mg	Total Fat: 0	Monounsaturated Fat: 0

Diabetic Exchange: Substitute sugar-free maple syrup and count 1 tablespoon as free food.

FRESH CORN GRIDDLECAKES
"With homemade, non-fat maple syrup!"

1 1/4 cups flour
1 teaspoon baking powder
1/8 teaspoon salt
egg substitute equivalent to
   2 eggs
1 cup evaporated skim milk
2 tablespoons corn oil

2 cups corn, cut from cob
no-stick cooking spray, for griddle
SYRUP:
1 cup water
2 cups sugar
1/2 teaspoon maple flavoring
1/8 teaspoon cinnamon

Sift the first 3 ingredients; set aside. Combine the next 3 ingredients and mix with the flour mixture; stir in corn. Drop by spoonfuls onto a preheated, lightly sprayed griddle. Cook as you would regular pancakes. Serve hot with light margarine or maple syrup. Yields 12 4-inch griddlecakes.

Recipe continues on page 19.

SYRUP: In medium saucepan bring water to boil; add sugar, flavoring and cinnamon. Cook 2–3 minutes, stirring constantly. Yields 1 1/2 cups.

VARIATION: 2 cups canned small-kernel white or yellow corn can be substituted in this recipe. If using canned corn, drain, place on cutting board and chop coarsely before adding to recipe.

Note: When cutting the corn from the cob, split each row of corn and scrape corn and juice into a bowl. Be careful not to use large kernels of corn. Fresh, small-kernel corn is best in this recipe.

"Serve for breakfast or dinner!"

Nutritional Analysis Per Griddlecake without Syrup or Margarine

Calories: 115	Protein: 5 g	Saturated Fat: 0.4 g
Cholesterol: 1 mg	Carbohydrate: 18 g	Polyunsaturated Fat: 1.7g
Sodium: 93 mg	Total Fat: 2.8 g	Monounsaturated Fat: 0.7 g

% of calories from fat = 22%

Diabetic Exchanges: 1 bread, 1/2 fat

Nutritional Analysis Per Tablespoon of Syrup

Calories: 30	Protein: 0	Saturated Fat: 0
Cholesterol: 0	Carbohydrate: 8	Polyunsaturated Fat: 0
Sodium: 0	Total Fat: 0	Monounsaturated Fat: 0

(Syrup is not appropriate for diabetic diet. Try a sugarfree maple syrup.)

HOMEMADE BANANA NUT BREAD
"Moist and delicious!"

1/4 cup corn oil margarine, softened
1 cup sugar
egg substitute equivalent to 2 eggs
2 cups all-purpose flour
1 teaspoon baking soda
1/4 teaspoon cinnamon

1/8 teaspoon nutmeg
4 medium-large, over-ripe bananas, mashed
1/4 cup chopped pecans or walnuts
no-stick cooking spray

Preheat oven to 350. With electric mixer on medium speed, cream margarine with sugar until thoroughly creamed. Add egg substitute, mix until well blended. Sift the next 4 ingredients together; add to creamed mixture, alternating with mashed bananas. Stir in nuts. DO NOT OVERMIX. Spray loaf pan (approximately 8×4); pour in batter. Bake for 55–60 minutes or until just done. DO NOT OVERBAKE! Allow bread to cool completely in pan before slicing. Yields 16 slices.

NOTE: Double the recipe; bake two and freeze one! Remove from pan before freezing!

BANANA NOTE: Over-ripe bananas can be frozen in the skin until ready to make bread. Peel while frozen; place in bowl to defrost. Mash when soft.

"The secret to the moist banana bread is the over-ripe bananas!"

Nutritional Analysis Per Slice

Calories: 172	Protein: 3 g	Saturated Fat: 0.9 g
Cholesterol: 0 mg	Carbohydrate: 31 g	Polyunsaturated Fat: 1.1 g
Sodium: 99 mg	Total Fat: 4.5 g	Monounsaturated Fat: 2.5 g

% of calories from fat = 24%

(Not appropriate for diabetic diets.)

APRICOT MUFFINS
"Good for breakfast, lunch or tea!"

1 12-ounce package dried apricots
1 cup sugar
2 tablespoons margarine
egg substitute equivalent to 1 egg
1/4 cup water
1/2 cup orange juice

2 cups sifted flour
2 teaspoons baking powder
1/4 teaspoon baking soda
1/4 cup raisins
no-stick cooking spray

Cover apricots in warm water and let stand for 30 minutes; drain and cut into thin strips. Preheat oven to 350. Cream sugar and margarine; add egg substitute, water and orange juice. Mix flour, baking powder and baking soda; gradually add to creamed mixture. Stir in apricots and raisins. Spray 12 muffin tins; spoon batter into tins, using all of the batter. Bake for 30 minutes. Remove from oven and cool. Store in a tightly sealed container or freeze. Yields 12 regular muffins or 36 miniature muffins (see note).

NOTE: To make 36 miniature muffins, spray mini-muffin tins and spoon batter into tins, using all of the batter. Bake for 22–24 minutes or until center springs back when pressed gently.

"Great for breakfast-on-the-run since your bread and fruit are all in one! An apricot lover's treat!"

Nutritional Analysis Per Regular Muffin (Per Miniature Muffin)

Calories: 236 (79)	Protein: 4 (1) g	Saturated Fat: 0.5 (0.1) g
Cholesterol: 0 (0)	Carbohydrate: 52 (17) g	Polyunsaturated Fat: 1.0 (0.3) g
Sodium: 92 (31) mg	Total Fat: 2.8 (0.9) g	Monounsaturated Fat: 1.3 (0.5) g

% of calories from fat = 10 (10) %

Diabetic Exchanges: Not appropriate for diabetic diet (1 mini-muffin for occasional use = 1 bread)

POPOVER MUFFINS
"Serve hot from the oven!"

no-stick cooking spray
fat-free egg substitute equivalent to 1 egg
2 egg whites, beaten slightly
1 cup CalciMilk
    or
1 cup 1% low-fat milk

1 cup flour
1/4 tablespoon salt
1 tablespoon canola oil
1/8 teaspoon dry mustard

Preheat oven to 475. Spray 12 muffin tins; set aside. Combine eggs, milk, flour and salt; beat with electric mixer or food processor until frothy, about 1 1/2 minutes. Add oil and dry mustard; beat only 30 seconds more. Pour batter into the muffin tins. Bake 15 minutes; then reduce heat to 350 and bake for another 20 minutes, or until firm and browned. A few minutes before popovers are completely cooked, pierce top or side of each with a sharp knife to let the steam escape. Yields 12 muffins.

Recipe continues on page 21.

Note: If you prefer drier popovers, leave them in the oven with the oven door open for 20 minutes after the heat has been turned off. CalciMilk is a high calcium 1% lactaid milk; if not available, use 1% milk.

"Toasted Popover Muffins are delicious for breakfast or for lunch with a cup of soup!"

Nutritional Analysis Per Muffin

Calories: 58	Protein: 3 g	Saturated Fat: 0.2 g
Cholesterol: 1 mg	Carbohydrate: 9 g	Polyunsaturated Fat: 0.3 g
Sodium: 66 mg	Total Fat: 1.1 g	Monounsaturated Fat: 0.6 g

% of calories from fat = 17%

Diabetic Exchange: 1/2 bread

DOUBLE CORN BREAD WITH CHEDDAR
"A Southwest flavor!"

no-stick cooking spray
1/4 cup green pepper
1/4 cup sweet red pepper
1/4 cup jalapeño pepper
3/4 cup fresh or canned small-kernel corn
1 cup all purpose flour, divided
1 cup white or yellow corn meal, preferably stone ground
2 teaspoons baking powder

1/2 teaspoon baking soda
1 cup buttermilk
egg substitute equivalent to 3 eggs
1/4 teaspoon freshly ground black pepper
1/8–1/4 teaspoon cayenne pepper
1/8 teaspoon dry mustard
2 tablespoons canola oil
1/4 cup grated reduced-fat Cheddar cheese

Preheat oven to 400. Spray an 8x4 loaf pan and set aside. Seed and chop 3 kinds of peppers; dust peppers and corn lightly with 1 tablespoon flour and set aside. Combine remaining flour, corn meal, baking powder and soda; mix well. Quickly stir in combined liquid ingredients; fold in peppers and all remaining ingredients. Spoon into loaf pan and bake 40–45 minutes, or until cake tester comes out clean. Let the bread rest 5 minutes before removing from pan; cool on a wire rack. Wrap and allow flavors to ripen for 24 hours before slicing. Yields 18 thin slices.

Note: Slice with a serrated knife and toast for peak flavor! If made more than one day ahead, keep in refrigerator.

"Serve toasted slices with soup and chili!"

Nutritional Analysis Per Slice

Calories: 93	Protein: 4 g	Saturated Fat: 0.5 g
Cholesterol: 2 mg	Carbohydrate: 14 g	Polyunsaturated Fat: 0.9 g
Sodium: 132 mg	Total Fat: 2.5 g	Monounsaturated Fat: 1.1 g

% of calories from fat = 24%

Diabetic Exchanges: 1 bread, 1/2 fat

BROCCOLI STIR FRY
"Tender crisp!"

1 teaspoon sesame seeds
1/3 cup low-sodium chicken broth, defatted
3/4 teaspoon cornstarch
1 teaspoon minced fresh ginger root
2 teaspoons reduced-sodium soy sauce

1 teaspoon corn oil
1/2 teaspoon finely chopped garlic
1 pound broccoli, cut into flowerets
   (approximately 3–3 1/2 cups)

Preheat oven to 350. Place the sesame seeds in the preheated oven and toast until a golden brown, about 5 minutes. Watch carefully, as they burn easily. Set aside. Combine chicken broth and cornstarch and mix until cornstarch is dissolved. Add ginger and soy sauce. Mix well and set aside. Heat oil in a wok or large skillet. Add garlic and cook until it sizzles; do not brown. Add broccoli and toss for one minute. Restir chicken broth mixture and pour over broccoli; cover and cook for 3–4 minutes or until just tender. Add toasted sesame seeds and mix well. Yields 4 servings.

Note: Peeled broccoli stems can be cut into paper-thin circles and stir-fried with the flowerets.

"Serve with grilled seafood!"

Nutritional Analysis Per Serving

Calories: 52	Protein: 4 g	Saturated Fat: 0.3 g
Cholesterol: 0	Carbohydrate: 7 g	Polyunsaturated Fat: 1.2 g
Sodium: 131 mg	Total Fat: 2.0 g	Monounsaturated Fat: 0.5 g

Note: A portion of food containing 3 grams or less of fat is considered a low-fat serving.
Diabetic Exchanges: 1 vegetable, 1/2 fat

HOT STRING BEANS
"Can also be served cold!"

1 1/2 pounds fresh green beans
1 10-ounce can low-sodium beef broth,
   defatted
1/2 cup diced onions
1 1/2 tablespoons extra-virgin olive oil
   or canola oil
2 tablespoons red wine vinegar

1 cup reserved bean cooking liquid
2 teaspoons sugar
1/8 teaspoon Hungarian sweet
   paprika
GARNISH:
2 tablespoons chopped green onions
1 pint cherry tomatoes, halved

Clean green beans; remove strings and cut into serving size pieces. Bring beef broth to a boil; add beans and cook 5–7 minutes or until beans are tender, but still crisp.

Recipe continues on page 23.

RESERVE ONE CUP OF COOKING LIQUID; strain and set aside. Combine all remaining ingredients except green onions; add reserved broth and pour over hot beans. Serve hot, at room temperature or chill and serve cold. When ready to serve, garnish with green onions and cherry tomatoes. Serves 6.

NOTE: Frozen cut green beans can be used. Follow cooking directions.

"Delicious with roasted meats or chicken and baked potatoes!"

Nutritional Analysis Per Serving with Garnish

Calories: 83	Protein: 3 g	Saturated Fat: 0.6 g
Cholesterol: 0	Carbohydrate: 14 g	Polyunsaturated Fat: 0.5 g
Sodium: 7 mg	Total Fat: 2.9 g	Monounsaturated Fat: 1.8 g

Note: A portion of food containing 3 grams or less of fat is considered a low-fat serving.
Diabetic Exchanges: 1 bread, 1/2 fat

ZUCCHINI-TOMATO SUPREME
"A robust Italian flavor!"

2 medium-large zucchini, sliced into
    8 half-inch slices (reserve small
    ends for other uses)
1/4 teaspoon salt
1/4 teaspoon garlic powder
1 quart water
no-sticking cooking spray
4 medium tomatoes, peeled and
    sliced into 8 half-inch slices
1 tablespoon minced fresh basil
    or
1 teaspoon dried basil

1 tablespoon fresh oregano, minced
    or
1 teaspoon dried oregano
1/4 teaspoon cracked black pepper
1/2 tablespoon canola oil
    or
1/2 tablespoon extra-virgin olive oil
8 teaspoons freshly grated Parmesan
    cheese
2 ounces part-skim milk mozzarella
    cheese, grated

Preheat oven to 350. Place zucchini, salt and garlic powder in a saucepan; cover with water and cook until barely fork tender. Drain on toweling. Spray a 7×11 glass baking dish; place 8 zucchini slices in bottom of dish and top with 8 tomato slices. Sprinkle with basil, oregano and pepper; drizzle with oil. Top with Parmesan cheese and bake uncovered for 20–25 minutes; remove from oven. Top with mozzarella and place under broiler until cheese melts. Serves 8.

Note: Freshly grated Parmesan cheese should be used in this recipe. The flavor is worth the difference!

"Best when tomatoes and zucchini are at their peak flavor!"

Nutritional Analysis Per Serving

Calories: 60	Protein: 4 g	Saturated Fat: 1.4 g
Cholesterol: 6 mg	Carbohydrate: 5 g	Polyunsaturated Fat: 0.2 g
Sodium: 140 mg	Total Fat: 2.9 g	Monounsaturated Fat: 1.3 g

Note: A portion of food containing 3 grams or less of fat is considered a low-fat serving.
Diabetic Exchanges: 1 vegetable, 1/2 fat

VEGETABLE LASAGNA
"Made with uncooked noodles!"

no-stick cooking spray
6 uncooked lasagna noodles (DO NOT COOK)
5 cups (1 1/4 pounds) thinly-sliced zucchini
1 1/4 cups shredded part-skim mozzarella cheese, divided, for topping
2 tablespoons freshly grated Parmesan cheese, for topping

SPINACH FILLING:
1 10-ounce package frozen chopped spinach, thawed and drained
1 12-ounce carton 1% low-fat cottage cheese
egg substitute equivalent to 1 egg, beaten

TOMATO SAUCE:
2 teaspoons extra-virgin olive oil
3/4 cup minced onion
1 cup sliced mushrooms
2 cloves garlic, minced
2 14 1/2-ounce cans no-salt-added tomatoes, drained and chopped
1/4 cup minced fresh parsley
1 tablespoon red wine vinegar
3 tablespoons beef broth
1/4 cup tomato paste
2 teaspoons fresh basil, minced
1 1/2 teaspoons fresh oregano, minced
1 teaspoon brown sugar
1/2 teaspoon pepper
1/4 teaspoon salt

Prepare zucchini and cheeses; set aside: Press spinach between paper towels to remove all water. Combine spinach, cottage cheese, and egg substitute; set aside. Sauté onion in oil; add remaining tomato sauce ingredients. Reduce heat and simmer, uncovered, for 20 minutes; set aside. Coat a 9×13 glass baking dish with cooking spray. Spoon one-third tomato mixture into baking dish. Arrange 3 uncooked noodles lengthwise; top with 1 1/4 cups spinach mixture, 2 1/2 cups zucchini, and 1/2 cup mozzarella. Repeat layers; top with remaining tomato mixture. Cover and refrigerate 8 hours. Bake, covered, at 350 for 1 1/2 hours. Uncover and sprinkle with remaining 1/4 cup mozzarella and Parmesan cheese. Let stand 5 minutes before serving. Yields 8 3×4-inch servings.

NOTE: *Remember not to cook the noodles; they cook during the 1 1/2-hour cooking time. If dried herbs are used, use half the amount specified in recipe.*

"Serve as a vegetable or a meatless entrée!"

Nutritional Analysis Per Serving

Calories: 221	Protein: 17 g	Saturated Fat: 3.0 g
Cholesterol: 13 mg	Carbohydrate: 27 g	Polyunsaturated Fat: 0.6 g
Sodium: 424 mg	Total Fat: 6.0 g	Monounsaturated Fat: 2.4 g

% of calories from fat = 24%
Diabetic Exchanges: 2 lean meats, 2 breads

SPICY RED CABBAGE
"Serve with pork or game!"

1 3-pound head red cabbage	1/2 teaspoon seasoned salt
no-stick cooking spray	2/3 cup red currant jelly
1 large red onion, chopped	or
2 cups tart apples, peeled and diced	2/3 cup currant jelly
1/2 cup red wine vinegar	2 slices bacon, cooked and
1/2 teaspoon caraway seed	crumbled (optional)
2 heaping tablespoons dark brown sugar	

Remove outer leaves from cabbage and save for other use; thinly slice remaining cabbage. Spray a large pot and sauté onion until soft. Add cabbage and cook uncovered over low heat for 15 minutes; stir cabbage every 5 minutes. Add apples, vinegar, caraway seeds, brown sugar and seasoned salt. Cover and cook over low heat for 1 hour and 15 minutes; stir several times. Stir in jelly and cook an additional 15 minutes. Place in serving bowl; sprinkle with crumbled bacon, if desired. Serve warm. Serves 12. Best made one day ahead. Do not add bacon until ready to serve.

NOTE: If prepared a day ahead, warm over low heat when ready to serve. To lower sodium content, reduce amount of seasoned salt.

"Tart and spicy!"

Nutritional Analysis Per Serving without Bacon (with Bacon)

Calories: 104 (110)	Protein: 2 (2) g	Saturated Fat: 0.1 (0.3) g
Cholesterol: 0 (1) mg	Carbohydrate: 27 (27) g	Polyunsaturated Fat: 0.2 (0.3) g
Sodium: 99 (116) mg	Total Fat: 0.4 (0.9) g	Monounsaturated Fat: 0.1 (0.3) g

% of calories from fat = 4 (8) %
(Not appropriate for diabetic diets)

 VEGETABLE IDEAS

LEMON HONEY CARROTS: Top hot cooked carrots with a blend of 1 1/2 teaspoons honey, 1 teaspoon Dijon mustard, 1/2 teaspoon lemon juice and 1/4 teaspoon grated lemon peel.

PICKLED BEETS: Simmer canned small whole beets for 5 minutes with 3/4 cup vinegar, 1 teaspoon pickling spices, 1 cinnamon stick and 2–3 teaspoons sugar or equivalent amount sugar substitute; place in glass jar and chill for 2–3 days before serving.

OVEN-BAKED PARMESAN RICE
"Serve with roasted meats and seafood!"

no-stick cooking spray
2 tablespoons tub margarine
2 cloves garlic, minced
3 cups uncooked long-grain white rice
1/2 cup water
2 10 3/4-ounce cans low-sodium beef
  broth, defatted

2 10 3/4-ounce cans low-sodium chicken
  broth, defatted
1 tablespoon white wine vinegar
1/4 teaspoon dry mustard
1/8 teaspoon cayenne pepper
1/2 cup freshly grated Parmesan cheese

Preheat oven to 375. Spray a 9×13 glass baking dish with no-stick cooking spray; add margarine and garlic. Place in oven for 3–5 minutes or until margarine is melted and garlic is light golden brown. DO NOT OVERBROWN! Place rice in dish; toss to coat. Add all remaining ingredients; mix and cover dish with foil. Bake covered for 20 minutes; stir, recover and continue baking for 25–30 minutes or until rice is fluffy and all liquid has been absorbed. Serves 12.

Note: This recipe is a buffet dream since it can wait in a turned-off oven up to 30 minutes until your guests finally get to dinner! For smaller groups, cook the entire recipe; place leftover rice in plastic bag to reheat. Cooked rice can also be frozen.

"Use only Parmesan cheese that you have freshly grated. The flavor is worth it!"

Nutritional Analysis Per Serving

Calories: 208	Protein: 5 g	Saturated Fat: 1.3 g
Cholesterol: 3 mg	Carbohydrate: 38 g	Polyunsaturated Fat: 1.0 g
Sodium: 104 mg	Total Fat: 3.5 g	Monounsaturated Fat: 1.2 g

% of calories from fat = 16%
Diabetic Exchanges: 2 1/2 breads, 1/2 fat

PINEAPPLE RICE

Mix hot rice with lightly drained crushed pineapple. For a delicious fat-free rice dish, don't add oil or margarine! Serve with roasted poultry, pork and game.

MASHED POTATOES
"Rich and creamy!"

1 chicken bouillon cube
6 medium potatoes, pared
1/4 cup chopped onions
1/4 teaspoon minced garlic

2 tablespoons light sour cream
GARNISH:
1 teaspoon minced fresh parsley
1/8 teaspoon cracked black pepper

Place first 4 ingredients in a medium saucepan; cover with water. Bring to boil; reduce heat to simmer and cook, covered, until potatoes are very tender. Discard strained cooking broth and place potatoes and remaining pieces of onion and garlic in small mixing bowl; add sour cream and beat with electric mixer until smooth and creamy. Garnish with minced parsley and cracked black pepper. Serves 4.

NOTE: Prepare ahead of time and reheat in the microwave.

"Delicious with roasted meats or grilled seafood!'"

Nutritional Analysis Per Serving

Calories: 193	Protein: 4 g	Saturated Fat: 0.3 g
Cholesterol: 2 mg	Carbohydrate: 42 g	Polyunsaturated Fat: 0.6 g
Sodium: 122 mg	Total Fat: 1.0 g	Monounsaturated Fat: 0.1 g
	% of calories from fat = 5%	
	Diabetic Exchange: 3 breads	

SPRINGTIME POTATOES

Top hot boiled new potatoes with a small amount of tub margarine mixed with fresh parsley, fresh mint leaves and a pinch of nutmeg. Ah! Springtime!

SWEET POTATO CASSEROLE
"Topped with golden marshmallows!"

2 pounds sweet potatoes
1/2 cup light brown sugar
2 tablespoons corn oil margarine
egg substitute equivalent to 1 egg
1/4 teaspoon cinnamon

1/4 teaspoon nutmeg
1/8 teaspoon salt
2/3 cup evaporated skim milk
no-stick cooking spray, for dish
1 cup miniature marshmallows

Cook unpeeled potatoes in boiling water; when cool, peel and mash. Combine all ingredients except the marshmallows and cooking spray. Lightly spray a 1 1/2-quart casserole. Spoon mixture into casserole. Top with marshmallows and bake in a preheated 350-degree oven for 25–30 minutes or until the marshmallows are golden brown. Serves 8.

Note: Depending on the moisture in the potatoes, it may be necessary to add 1–2 tablespoons evaporated skim milk.

"This dish can be prepared a day ahead and baked just before serving."

Nutritional Analysis Per Serving

Calories: 248	Protein: 6 g	Saturated Fat: 1 g
Cholesterol: 1 mg	Carbohydrate: 49 g	Polyunsaturated Fat: 1 g
Sodium: 137 mg	Total Fat: 4 g	Monounsaturated Fat: 2 g
	% of calories from fat = 13%	
	(Not appropriate for diabetic diets)	

CRAB IMPERIAL
"A classic crab dish for a heart-healthy diet!"

1 pound regular or backfin crab meat
1 tablespoon chopped fresh parsley
2 tablespoons pimento, drained and
  chopped
1-2 teaspoons capers, drained and
  chopped
1/4-1/2 teaspoon dry mustard

2 tablespoons reduced-calorie
  mayonnaise
2 tablespoons fat-free mayonnaise
  dressing
1/4 cup fat-free sour cream
1 teaspoon Parmesan cheese, for
  garnish

Preheat oven to 350. Carefully pick through crab to remove all shell; set aside. Combine next 7 ingredients and spoon over crab; mix gently. Do not break apart lumps of crab. Spoon mixture into 6 individual baking shells or individual baking dishes; top with cheese. Bake for 20–22 minutes or until golden brown around the edges. DO NOT OVERBAKE. Serves 6.

NOTE: Prepare early in the day and chill until ready to bake.

"An outstanding seafood dish!"

Nutritional Analysis Per Serving

Calories: 101	Protein: 14 g	Saturated Fat: 2.0 g
Cholesterol: 78 mg	Carbohydrate: 3 g	Polyunsaturated Fat: 0
Sodium: 364 mg	Total Fat: 2.9 g	Monounsaturated Fat: 0.9 g

% of calories from fat = 26%
Diabetic Exchanges: 1 vegetable, 2 lean meats

CRAB APPETIZER PIE

Follow directions above for preparing Crab Imperial; bake in a shallow 8-inch pie plate or quiche dish for 25–30 minutes or until golden brown. Serve with unsalted plain melba rounds. Yields 20–25 servings.

STIR-FRIED SHRIMP AND RICE
"Cooks in less than 10 minutes!"

no-stick cooking spray
1 tablespoon tub margarine
1 pound uncooked shrimp, shelled and
  cleaned
1/2 cup chopped onion
1/4 cup chopped green pepper
1/4 cup chopped sweet red pepper
2 cloves garlic, minced
1 teaspoon low-sodium chicken bouillon
  granules

1/4 teaspoon dry mustard
1/8 teaspoon ground ginger
egg substitute equivalent to 2 eggs
3 cups cooked rice
1–2 tablespoons reduced-sodium soy
  sauce
1/8 teaspoon fresh cracked pepper
1–2 tablespoons minced green onions,
  for garnish

Spray a 10-inch skillet with no-stick cooking spray; add margarine and melt. Add shrimp and stir-fry over medium-high heat only until shrimp turns pink. Remove shrimp from pan and set aside. Place onion and peppers in pan and stir-fry for 2 minutes; add garlic, chicken granules, mustard and ginger, and stir-fry for 1 minute. Stir in egg substitute and stir-fry for 2 minutes; add rice and shrimp and stir for 1–2 minutes or until heated through. Remove from heat; season with soy sauce and pepper. Place shrimp and rice on serving dish; top with green onions. Serves 6.

"Perfect for today's busy cooks!"

Nutritional Analysis Per Serving

Calories: 199	Protein: 13 g	Saturated Fat: 0.7 g
Cholesterol: 66 mg	Carbohydrate: 28 g	Polyunsaturated Fat: 1.3 g
Sodium: 211 mg	Total Fat: 3.1 g	Monounsaturated Fat: 1.1 g

% of calories from fat = 19%

Diabetic Exchanges: 3 breads, 1 1/2 lean meats

SHRIMP AND CRAB CASSEROLE
"Great for entertaining!"

12 ounces crab meat, preferably backfin
1 cup cooked shrimp, peeled,
   deveined and chopped
1/2 small onion, finely chopped
1/4 cup chopped celery
1/4 cup chopped green pepper
1/4 cup reduced-calorie mayonnaise
1/4 cup plain fat-free sour cream

1/2 teaspoon lemon juice
1/2 teaspoon reduced-sodium
   Worcestershire sauce
1/8 teaspoon dry mustard
1/8 teaspoon freshly cracked pepper
no-stick cooking spray
1/2 cup soft whole wheat bread crumbs
   (made from low-fat bread)

Gently pick through crab to remove all shell. Do not break apart lumps of crab. Set crab and shrimp aside. Combine all remaining ingredients except bread crumbs in a large bowl; gently fold in seafood. Spoon into an uncovered, lightly sprayed 1 1/2-quart casserole. Sprinkle bread crumbs over casserole. Bake in a preheated 350-degree oven for 25 minutes or until browned on top. Serves 6.

"Nice for a small buffet dinner party!"

Nutritional Analysis Per Serving

Calories: 147	Protein: 20 g	Saturated Fat: 1.5 g
Cholesterol: 128 mg	Carbohydrate: 5 g	Polyunsaturated Fat: 3.2 g
Sodium: 308 mg	Total Fat: 4.7 g	Monounsaturated Fat: 0

% of calories from fat = 29%

Diabetic Exchanges: 2 1/2 lean meats, 1 vegetable

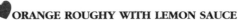

ORANGE ROUGHY WITH LEMON SAUCE
Top broiled orange roughy fillets with 1 teaspoon lemon sauce made by combining 1 tablespoon tub margarine, 1 1/2 teaspoons fresh lemon juice, 1/4 teaspoon grated lemon rind, 1 tablespoon minced parsley or chives and 2–3 shakes of hot pepper sauce. Zesty!

BROILED FILLET OF SALMON
"Topped with cucumber mint sauce!"

4 4-ounce pieces of salmon fillet
2 teaspoons corn oil margarine,
    softened
1–2 teaspoons fresh lemon juice
4 cups cooked brown rice
CUCUMBER MINT SAUCE:
4 tablespoons fat-free sour cream
4 teaspoons fat-free
    mayonnaise dressing

1 1/4 teaspoons chopped fresh mint
4 tablespoons minced cucumbers
1/4 teaspoon fresh lemon juice
GARNISH:
4–6 cucumber slices
1/4 teaspoon freshly ground pepper
1 teaspoon chopped green onions with
    tops

Place fillets in broiling pan; top each fillet with 1/4 teaspoon margarine. Broil 5 minutes; turn fillets and top with 1/4 teaspoon margarine and 1/4–1/2 teaspoon lemon juice. Broil an additional 3–5 minutes depending on thickness of fillet. Place 1 cup rice on individual serving plate; top with fillet and 1–2 tablespoons sauce. Garnish each serving with a cucumber slice, pepper and green onions. Serves 4.

CUCUMBER MINT SAUCE: Combine 5 sauce ingredients while fish is broiling.

"The sauce is also delicious on grilled mackerel or tuna steaks!"

Nutritional Analysis Per Serving with 1 Cup of Rice and 1 Tablespoon of Sauce

Calories: 383	Protein: 25 g	Saturated Fat: 2.0 g
Cholesterol: 64 mg	Carbohydrate: 47 g	Polyunsaturated Fat: 3.1 g
Sodium: 83 mg	Total Fat: 10.6 g	Monounsaturated Fat: 5.5 g

% of calories from fat = 25%
Diabetic Exchanges: 3 breads, 2 1/2 lean meats, 1 fat

FILLET OF FISH MEXICALI
"Baked with fresh tomato salsa!"

4 3–4-ounce pieces fish fillets; use
    flounder, halibut, cod, pompano or sole
3 cups cooked rice, for serving
SALSA:
no-stick cooking spray
1–2 cloves garlic, minced
1 onion, chopped
1/4 cup chopped green pepper
1/4 cup chopped celery
1–2 tablespoons pimento-stuffed green
    olives, sliced
1/2 cup diced red-ripe plum tomatoes or
    drained and chopped canned tomatoes
1/2 cup tomato sauce
1 tablespoon minced fresh parsley

1/2 teaspoon fresh lemon juice
1/2 teaspoon fresh lime juice
1/4–1/2 teaspoon ground cumin
1–2 tablespoons canned green chilies,
    chopped (hot or mild)
1 tablespoon capers
1 tablespoon minced fresh cilantro
    or
1 teaspoon dried cilantro
up to 1/4 cup water or tomato juice
    (optional)
GARNISH:
1 lemon, sliced
1 teaspoon minced fresh cilantro or
    parsley

Spray a large teflon-coated skillet; sauté garlic and onion over medium heat until light golden. Add next 5 salsa ingredients; bring to boil. Add all remaining salsa ingredients; stir to mix well. Allow to simmer for 30 minutes. Place half of the salsa in

Recipe continues to page 31.

a flat baking dish; top with fillets and cover with remaining salsa. Bake uncovered in a preheated 350-degree oven for 25–30 minutes or until fish flakes easily when touched with a fork. Serves 4.

TO SERVE: Place hot rice on a serving plate; top with fillet and salsa sauce. Garnish with lemon slices and cilantro or parsley.

"Deliciously spicy and wonderfully healthy!"

Nutritional Analysis Per Serving

Calories: 324	Protein: 21 g	Saturated Fat: 1.0 g
Cholesterol: 0	Carbohydrate: 53 g	Polyunsaturated Fat: 1.3 g
Sodium: 311 mg	Total Fat: 3.3 g	Monounsaturated Fat: 1.0 g
	% of calories from fat = 9%	

Diabetic Exchange: 3 breads, 2 lean meats, 1 vegetable

SEAFOOD SUGGESTIONS

BROILED CATFISH WITH SAUCE: Top broiled catfish fillets with 1 tablespoon spicy creole sauce or spicy tomato salsa. Great taste!

GRILLED HALIBUT: Top grilled halibut fillets or steaks with a 1-tablespoon mixture of diced fresh tomatoes, fresh basil, olive oil and cracked pepper. Mouthwatering!

BARBECUED SWORDFISH OR HALIBUT STEAKS
"Uses your favorite barbecue sauce!"

4 swordfish or halibut steaks
1 1/3 teaspoons canola or peanut oil
1 teaspoon fresh lemon juice
1 teaspoon cracked black pepper
1/2 teaspoon Dijon mustard
1/8 teaspoon hot pepper sauce
1/2 cup barbecue sauce of your choice

GARNISH:
1 lemon, sliced
1 mild onion, sliced
4–8 sprigs parsley
GRILLED VEGETABLES:
4 cups sliced yellow squash or zucchini
1/4 cup fat-free Italian dressing

Rinse steaks; dry well and set aside until ready to cook. Combine oil, lemon juice, pepper, mustard and hot pepper sauce; mix well. Place steaks over a moderately hot fire; brush lightly with oil mixture. Grill 3–5 inches from heat for 5–8 minutes depending on thickness of steaks. Turn steaks; brush again with oil mixture and cook an additional 4–6 minutes or until fish separates easily when probed with a fork. Do not overcook! During last 2 minutes of cooking time, brush top side of each steak with 1 tablespoon barbecue sauce. Remove steaks from grill; place on platter, top side down, and brush each underside with 1 tablespoon of sauce. Garnish each steak with sliced lemons, onions and parsley; serve with additional barbecue sauce and grilled vegetables. Serves 4.

GRILLED VEGETABLES: While steaks are cooking, place vegetables on grill; brush with dressing. Cook 3–5 minutes per side or until fork tender.

"A man's seafood dish!"

Nutritional Analysis Per Fish Steak with 1 Cup of Vegetables

Calories: 209	Protein: 25 g	Saturated Fat: 1.5 g
Cholesterol: 44 mg	Carbohydrate: 13 g	Polyunsaturated Fat: 1.8 g
Sodium: 577 mg	Total Fat: 7.0 g	Monounsaturated Fat: 3.7 g
	% of calories from fat = 30%	

Diabetic Exchange: 3 lean meats, 3 vegetables

ITALIAN CHICKEN AND PASTA
"Cooked in a sensational tomato and fresh herb sauce!"

SAUCE:
no-stick cooking spray
1 medium onion, finely chopped
1 red or green pepper, seeded and finely
  chopped
6 large mushrooms, thinly sliced
1/3 cup chicken broth
2 tablespoons red wine vinegar
1 28-ounce can chopped tomatoes,
  drained
1 8-ounce can tomato sauce
1 clove garlic, finely minced
1 teaspoon sugar
1/4 teaspoon salt
1/4 teaspoon cracked black pepper

CHICKEN AND HERBS:
2 whole skinless, boneless chicken
  breasts (about 1 pound), cut into
  1 1/2-inch cubes
1–2 tablespoons chopped fresh basil or
  1 teaspoon dried basil
1 tablespoon chopped fresh parsley
1 tablespoon chopped fresh sage
  leaves or 1/2 teaspoon crumbled
  dried sage
PASTA AND GARNISH:
1 pound linguine, cooked and drained
1 tablespoon freshly grated Parmesan
  cheese, for garnish (optional)
1–2 tablespoons chopped fresh parsley,
  for garnish

Spray a large non-stick skillet with cooking spray; sauté onion, pepper and mushrooms over medium heat for 6–7 minutes, until softened, stirring occasionally. Add chicken broth and vinegar; bring to a boil and allow to boil for 2 minutes. Add tomatoes, tomato sauce, garlic, sugar, salt and pepper; stir to combine. Bring to a second boil, cover, reduce heat and simmer for 25 minutes. Add chicken, stir, cover and continue cooking for 15 minutes, or until chicken is just tender. Add basil, parsley and sage, cover and simmer for 5 minutes. Toss hot pasta with the sauce; sprinkle with parsley and cheese if desired. Serves 6.

"Don't let the long list of ingredients scare you; the preparation is very easy!"

Nutritional Analysis Per Serving without Cheese

Calories: 393	Protein: 29 g	Saturated Fat: 1.4 g
Cholesterol: 49 mg	Carbohydrate: 62 g	Polyunsaturated Fat: 1.4 g
Sodium: 550 mg	Total Fat: 3.9 g	Monounsaturated Fat: 1.1 g
	% of calories from fat = 9%	

Diabetic Exchanges: 4 breads, 2 1/2 lean meats

CHICKEN FLORENTINE
"This is a simple, yet elegant dish!"

no-stick cooking spray
2 10-ounce packages chopped frozen
  spinach, cooked and drained
2 tablespoons corn oil margarine
3 tablespoons flour
1/2 teaspoon Ac'cent
1/8 teaspoon salt
1/4 teaspoon dry mustard

1/4–1/2 teaspoon cayenne pepper
2 cups evaporated skim milk
1/2 cup freshly grated Parmesan
  cheese
2 cups cooked chicken, in chunks
1–1 1/2 cups soft bread, torn into pieces
  and toasted lightly

Spray a 1 1/2-quart casserole dish with no-stick cooking spray and place spinach in bottom. Melt margarine in a saucepan and stir in flour; let bubble 1 minute, stirring constantly. Add spices and milk; stir constantly until mixture thickens. Add cheese and chicken. Pour chicken mixture over spinach; top with bread pieces. Bake at 350 for 20–25 minutes or until casserole is heated completely. Serves 6.

"Serve with Fresh Fruit Salad (page 10) for a buffet dinner!"

Nutritional Analysis Per Serving

Calories: 246	Protein: 23 g	Saturated Fat: 3.0 g
Cholesterol: 34 mg	Carbohydrate: 22 g	Polyunsaturated Fat: 1.3 g
Sodium: 575 mg	Total Fat: 8.0 g	Monounsaturated Fat: 3.7 g

% of calories from fat = 29%

Diabetic Exchanges: 1 bread, 1 vegetable, 2 1/2 lean meats

CHICKEN AND SAUSAGE JAMBALAYA
"Long, slow cooking is the secret to this Cajun-style dish!"

no-stick cooking spray
1 1/2 cups chopped onion
6 green onions, chopped
3 cloves garlic, minced
1 large green pepper, chopped
4 ribs celery, chopped
1 6-ounce can low-sodium tomato paste
1 14–16-ounce can stewed tomatoes, chopped (reserve liquid)
1 10-ounce can Ro-Tel tomatoes and green chilies, chopped (reserve liquid) (see note)
1/4 cup fresh minced parsley
2 bay leaves
1 teaspoon dried thyme leaves
1 teaspoon dried basil leaves
1/4 teaspoon dry mustard
1/4 teaspoon black pepper
1/4 cup Worcestershire sauce
3 cups low-sodium chicken broth, defatted and divided
1/4 pound lean pork sausage (hot or regular), cooked and crumbled
1/4 pound smoked sausage, cut in thin slices and cooked
2 cups cooked chicken, cubed
1 cup long grain rice, uncooked
GARNISH:
1 green pepper, sliced in circles
1/4 cup chopped green onion

Generously spray a Dutch oven or heavy covered skillet with no-stick spray; sauté onions, garlic, green pepper and celery until just tender. Add tomato paste and both tomatoes; cook uncovered on low heat for 20–30 minutes or until mixture thickens and color begins to brown slightly. Add the next 7 ingredients, 2 cups chicken broth, reserved tomato liquid, well-drained sausages and chicken; cook on low, covered, for 1 hour, stirring several times. At the end of 1 hour, add uncooked rice and remaining cup of broth. Cover and cook on low for 40–45 minutes or until rice is tender and most of liquid is absorbed. Spoon onto a large platter and garnish with green pepper circles and chopped green onions. Yields 10 cups.

Note: If Ro-Tel tomatoes are not used, double the amount of stewed tomatoes and add 4 ounces drained hot canned green chilies plus 1/2 teaspoon hot pepper sauce.

"A one-dish meal!"

Nutritional Analysis Per Cup

Calories: 213	Protein: 12 g	Saturated Fat: 3.0 g
Cholesterol: 28 mg	Carbohydrate: 28 g	Polyunsaturated Fat: 1.0 g
Sodium: 498 mg	Total Fat: 6.3 g	Monounsaturated Fat: 2.3 g

% of calories from fat = 27%

Diabetic Exchanges: 1 medium-fat meat, 1 1/2 breads, 1 vegetable

HEALTHY HEART

MUSTARD-GRILLED FLANK STEAK
"Terrific!"

1-pound flank steak
4 slices sourdough bread or
   French bread
MUSTARD SAUCE:
1/3 cup Dijon mustard
2 tablespoons reduced-sodium soy
   sauce

1 tablespoon non-fat plain yogurt
1 tablespoon dried thyme, crumbled
1 teaspoon minced fresh ginger
1/4 teaspoon cracked black
   pepper

Combine all sauce ingredients and brush on both sides of steak; wrap in plastic wrap and allow to marinate in the refrigerator for a minimum of 6 hours or overnight. Cook over a hot gas or charcoal fire for approximately 5–6 minutes per side. Cut on the diagonal in thin slices. Heap sliced flank steak and any meat juices on toasted bread for serving. Yields 4 3-ounce servings.

"Serve with a fresh green salad and roasted potatoes!"

Nutritional Analysis Per 3-Ounce Serving with 1 Slice of Bread

Calories: 277	Protein: 31 g	Saturated Fat: 3.3 g
Cholesterol: 69 mg	Carbohydrate: 19 g	Polyunsaturated Fat: 1.0 g
Sodium: 557 mg	Total Fat: 8.0 g	Monounsaturated Fat: 3.7 g

% of calories from fat = 26%
Diabetic Exchange: 3 lean meats, 1 1/2 starch

BUTTERFLIED LEG OF LAMB ON THE GRILL
"Served on a bed of minted rice!"

1 7-pound leg of lamb, butterflied
2 teaspoons extra-virgin olive oil
1/2 cup fresh lemon juice
2–4 cloves garlic, minced
1/4 cup chopped green onions
1/4 cup Worcestershire sauce
1–2 teaspoons cracked black pepper
1 tablespoon Dijon mustard

MINTED RICE:
6 cups cooked rice
1/2 teaspoon dry mustard
1/4 teaspoon cracked black pepper
2 tablespoons fresh mint, finely
   chopped
2 teaspoons extra-virgin olive oil
GARNISH:
1/4 cup mint jelly

Remove all excess fat and place butterflied leg of lamb in a 9 x 13 glass dish. Combine all remaining ingredients except minted rice; mix well and pour over lamb. Cover and marinate in refrigerator for 24 hours; turn several times. Place lamb over a hot fire to sear, reduce heat to low and cook 12–14 minutes on each side if a covered gas grill is used. If a charcoal fire is used, cook over a medium fire for a total cooking time of 30–45 minutes. Brush with marinade several times while grilling. Remove meat from fire; place on carving tray or platter. Let stand 10 minutes before slicing on a slight diagonal in thin slices. Serve on a bed of minted rice. Top each serving with a small amount of meat juices and mint jelly. Serves 12.

Recipe continues on page 35.

MINTED RICE: Top hot rice with all remaining ingredients; mix well and divide into 12 servings.

SPECIAL MEAT NOTES: Before cooking lamb, trim ALL excess fat. Place fat side down and cut deep gashes in thick sections of lamb to make meat of uniform thickness. Meat should lie flat.

Note: Don't be intimidated by the name "butterflied." This is as easy as a steak to prepare.

"A cookout specialty!"

Nutritional Analysis Per Serving With Rice and Mint Jelly

Calories: 336	Protein: 26 g	Saturated Fat: 4.9 g
Cholesterol: 80 mg	Carbohydrate: 31 g	Polyunsaturated Fat: 0.8 g
Sodium: 88 mg	Total Fat: 11.2 g	Monounsaturated Fat: 5.5 g

% of calories from fat = 30%

Diabetic Exchanges: 3 lean meats, 2 breads

BRAISED LAMB SHANKS
"Tender and flavorful!"

no-stick cooking spray
4 lamb shanks
1/4 teaspoon dry mustard
1/8 teaspoon freshly ground pepper
1/2 teaspoon dried leaf oregano
2 3/4 cups reduced-sodium chicken broth, defatted
2 bay leaves
1 1/2 cups chopped onions
1 1/2 cups carrots, cut in 1-inch cubes
3/4 cup celery, sliced
3–4 garlic cloves, minced

1 bay leaf
3–4 whole peppercorns
2 whole cloves
1–1 1/2 tablespoons flour
1–2 tablespoons water
8 ounces small fresh button mushrooms steamed in 1/4 cup reduced-sodium, defatted chicken broth
1 tablespoon red wine vinegar
GARNISH:
2–3 tablespoons fresh chopped parsley
freshly ground black pepper

Generously spray a heavy Dutch oven or heavy covered skillet; brown shanks on all sides. Drain on paper toweling; wipe pan with toweling. Return lamb to pan; add next 12 ingredients. Cover and cook over low heat for 1 1/2–2 hours or until lamb shanks are tender. Remove shanks from pan; skim off any excess fat from cooking liquid. Mix flour with water; add to Dutch oven to thicken sauce. Cook, stirring, until thickened. Add lamb shanks, mushrooms and red wine vinegar. Simmer 5–10 minutes. Serves 4. Garnish with fresh parsley and freshly ground pepper.

Note: Can be prepared a day ahead to chill and remove all fat. If preparing ahead, do not thicken sauce or add mushrooms until ready to serve.

"Serve with crusty bread, steamed brown rice and a leafy green salad!"

Nutritional Analysis Per Serving

Calories: 282	Protein: 34 g	Saturated Fat: 7.0 g
Cholesterol: 100 mg	Carbohydrate: 17 g	Polyunsaturated Fat: 1.2 g
Sodium: 110 mg	Total Fat: 8.8 g	Monounsaturated Fat: 0.6 g

% of calories from fat = 28%

Diabetic Exchanges: 1 bread, 4 lean meats

THE "ULTIMATE" BARBECUE
"Made with sliced pork tenderloin so it's extra low in fat!"

1 1/2 -2 pounds boneless pork
tenderloin
1/4 cup reduced-sodium soy sauce
1/4 cup cider vinegar

2 tablespoons dark brown sugar
2 tablespoons honey
2/3 cup spicy barbecue sauce

Rinse tenderloin and pat dry. Mix next 4 ingredients and pour over tenderloin in an 8-inch square dish. Cover with plastic wrap and marinate overnight. Turn several times while marinating. Preheat oven to 350. Pour off marinade and reserve. Spoon 1/4 cup marinade over top and bake for 30 minutes or until fork tender. Baste every 10 minutes with an additional tablespoon of marinade. Remove from oven and pour off all marinade. Brush tenderloin with barbecue sauce and bake an additional 10 minutes, basting several times during baking time. Chill before slicing. Slice into thin circles and top with sauce. Serve warmed or chilled. Serves 8.

Note: If tenderloin is in two smaller pieces, place side by side while baking.

"And you thought you couldn't have barbecue!"

Nutritional Analysis Per Serving 2 1/4 Ounces Pork with Sauce

Calories: 132	Protein: 19 g	Saturated Fat: 1.2 g
Cholesterol: 50 mg	Carbohydrate: 7 g	Polyunsaturated Fat: 0.6 g
Sodium: 363 mg	Total Fat: 3.4 g	Monounsaturated Fat: 1.6 g

% of calories from fat = 22%
Diabetic Exchanges: 1/2 fruit, 2 1/2 lean meats

**AS AN APPETIZER**

Serve thinly-sliced pork tenderloin with spicy brown mustard on party-size rye bread.

**FOR AN OLD-FASHIONED BARBECUE SUPPER**

Serve The "Ultimate" Barbecue with rolls, hot mustard, Molded Cole Slaw (page 10) and Hot Green Beans (page 22).

LEMON BARBECUED PORK CHOPS
"Topped with a light barbecue sauce and sliced lemons!"

no-stick cooking spray
6 center cut pork chops, approximately
1/2–3/4-inch thick (trim all fat)
6 lemon slices

1/2 cup ketchup
1/4 cup cider vinegar
1/4 cup water
2 heaping tablespoons dark brown sugar

Spray a non-stick teflon-coated skillet with no-stick cooking spray; heat pan and brown chops; drain completely. Place the chops in a baking dish and top with lemon

Recipe continues on page 37.

slices. Mix ketchup, vinegar, water and sugar; pour over chops. Cover tightly and bake at 350 degrees for 45 minutes. Serves 6.

"These can be prepared ahead of time and baked when ready to serve!"

Nutritional Analysis Per Serving

Calories: 158	Protein: 20 g	Saturated Fat: 1.2 g
Cholesterol: 66 mg	Carbohydrate: 11 g	Polyunsaturated Fat: 0.6 g
Sodium: 248 mg	Total Fat: 3.4 g	Monounsaturated Fat: 1.6 g

% of calories from fat = 19%

Diabetic Exchanges, decreasing brown sugar to 1 tablespoon which reduces calories to 144 and carbohydrate to 7: 1/2 fruit, 3 lean meats

ITALIAN-STYLE STUFFED PEPPERS
"Rice and meat make this a main dish!"

6 medium green peppers
1 pound extra-lean ground beef
1 cup chopped onion
2 cloves fresh garlic, minced
1 cup cooked rice (do not use quick-cooking rice)
1/4 teaspoon dry mustard

1/4 teaspoon freshly cracked black pepper
1/2 teaspoon dried Italian seasoning
1 16-ounce jar Italian cooking sauce
2 ounces grated part-skim milk mozzarella cheese

Cut off tops of peppers; remove seeds and membranes. Parboil for 5 minutes; invert shells on paper toweling to drain all water. Sauté beef, onion and garlic until tender; drain well on toweling. Combine beef mixture with all remaining ingredients except sauce and cheese. Fill peppers and place upright in an 8-inch square glass baking dish; top with sauce. Bake in a preheated 350-degree oven for 40–45 minutes; top with cheese and bake an additional 10–15 minutes. Serves 6.

"Easy and delicious!"

Nutritional Analysis Per Serving

Calories: 284	Protein: 23 g	Saturated Fat: 3.3 g
Cholesterol: 51 mg	Carbohydrate: 27 g	Polyunsaturated Fat: 2.1 g
Sodium: 461 mg	Total Fat: 9.6 g	Monounsaturated Fat: 4.2 g

% of calories from fat = 30%

Diabetic Exchanges: 2 medium-fat meats, 1 bread, 2 vegetables

A VEGETARIAN ENTRÉE

For a deliciously hearty meatless entrée, try the Vegetable Lasagna (page 24) . . . loaded with spinach and zucchini in a rich tomato sauce.

STUFFED SHELLS
"A hearty Italian specialty!"

8 jumbo pasta shells
CHEESE FILLING:
3/4 cup 1% cottage cheese
1 tablespoon light cream cheese
1–2 teaspoons oregano
MEAT SAUCE:
1/2 pound extra-lean ground beef
1 medium onion, chopped
2 cloves garlic, minced
1 15-ounce can unsalted tomato sauce
1/4 teaspoon Italian seasoning

1 tablespoon fresh basil, minced
or
1 teaspoon dried basil
1/4 teaspoon dry mustard
2 teaspoons sugar
1/2 teaspoon cracked black pepper
TOPPING:
8 teaspoons grated part-skim
mozzarella cheese
1 tablespoon freshly grated Parmesan
cheese

SHELLS: Cook shells until just flexible enough to fill. Do not overcook. Rinse shells in cold water and drain on toweling; set shells aside.

CHEESE FILLING: Prepare cheese filling by placing cottage cheese and next 2 ingredients in food processor; blend until satin smooth. Set cheese filling aside.

MEAT SAUCE: Brown beef, onion and garlic in ungreased teflon skillet; drain on toweling. Return meat mixture to skillet. Add all remaining ingredients except cheese; bring to a boil, cover and reduce heat immediately. Simmer for 15–20 minutes or until thickened to desired consistency.

TO ASSEMBLE: Fill shells using all cheese filling. Place shells in an 8×8 glass baking dish; spoon sauce around shells. Sprinkle with both cheeses. Bake uncovered in a preheated 350-degree oven for 15–20 minutes or until cheese melts and dish is completely heated. Yields 4 servings of 2 shells each.

NOTE: The filling for the shells is very soft. This dish can be prepared early in the day and baked at serving time.

"You'll love this heart-healthy version of a classic Italian dish!"

Nutritional Analysis Per 2-Shell Serving

Calories: 394	Protein: 30 g	Saturated Fat: 4.0 g
Cholesterol: 51 mg	Carbohydrate: 54 g	Polyunsaturated Fat: 1.2 g
Sodium: 294 mg	Total Fat: 6.5 g	Monounsaturated Fat: 1.3 g

% of calories from fat = 15%
Diabetic Exchanges: 2 1/2 lean meats, 2 vegetables, 3 breads

ENTRÉES

HUEVOS RANCHEROS

"Can you believe it? A classic 'egg' dish in a heart healthy book!"

8 8-inch flour tortillas, heated
1/4 cup chopped onions
1/4 cup chopped canned green chilies,
  drained
2 tablespoons water
no-stick cooking spray
fat-free egg substitute equivalent to 8 eggs
  (see page 4 for homemade egg
  substitute)

1–2 cups hot or mild salsa, warmed
1/4 cup fat-free sour cream
GARNISH:
1/2 cup finely cut green onions
1/4 cup black or green olives, chopped
1/4 cup diced tomatoes

In a large non-stick teflon-coated skillet steam onions and green chilies in 2 tablespoons water until tender; remove from pan and set aside. Spray skillet with no-stick spray; add egg substitute, onions and chilies to pan and stir very gently with a spatula or large spoon. Stir only when eggs are beginning to set; do not overstir. When eggs are just done, remove from heat.

TO ASSEMBLE: Heat flour tortillas by instructions below. Place a heated flat tortilla on a plate; place 1/8 of the egg mixture down one side of each tortilla. Top with 1–2 tablespoons salsa, and 1 1/2 teaspoons sour cream; roll each tortilla. Repeat for all tortillas. Place on a large platter; spoon additional salsa over tortillas and sprinkle with garnish. Serve hot. Yields 8 tortillas.

TO HEAT TORTILLAS: Place on a microwave-safe dish, cover with plastic wrap and heat at 80% power, just long enough to warm tortillas.

"Try these, you'll love them!"

Nutritional Analysis Per Filled Tortilla

Calories: 198	Protein: 13 g	Saturated Fat: 1.6 g
Cholesterol: 1 mg	Carbohydrate: 25 g	Polyunsaturated Fat: 3.5 g
Sodium: 417 mg	Total Fat: 6.7 g	Monounsaturated Fat: 1.6 g

% of calories from fat = 30%
Diabetic Exchanges: 1 bread, 1 lean meat, 2 vegetables, 1 fat

LIGHT DINNERS OR LATE-NIGHT SUPPERS

For delicious casual dining try the Marinated Steak Salad (page 13) or the Grilled Fajitas with Cherry Tomato Salsa (page 9).

HEALTHY HEART

BUTTERMILK PINEAPPLE SHERBET
"Refreshing and delicious!"

1 cup crushed pineapple, drained (use
   pineapple packed in juice)
3/4 cup sugar
2 tablespoons fresh lemon juice

2 cups buttermilk
1 egg white, at room temperature
8 whole strawberries, for garnish

Combine pineapple and sugar; add lemon juice and buttermilk. Mix until well blended; pour into a shallow stainless steel or glass dish. Freeze until firm and then remove from dish; place in mixing bowl and break up with a wooden spoon. Beat with electric mixer until smooth. Set bowl in refrigerator while preparing egg white. Place egg white in small mixing bowl; beat until holds peaks when beaters are removed. Fold stiffly-beaten egg white into pineapple mixture; blend well. Return to shallow dish, cover with plastic wrap and freeze. Serves 8.

TO SERVE: Remove from freezer and allow to soften for a minute or two before scooping into serving dishes. Garnish with strawberries or other fresh fruit.

"Use your favorite fruit to top off this sherbet and serve as a fresh fruit sundae!"

Nutritional Analysis Per Serving without Garnish

Calories: 113	Protein: 3 g	Saturated Fat: 0
Cholesterol: 2 mg	Carbohydrate: 26 g	Polyunsaturated Fat: 0
Sodium: 71 mg	Total Fat: 0	Monounsaturated Fat: 0

(Not appropriate for diabetic diet)

 SHERBET WITH FRUIT

*Top Buttermilk Pineapple Sherbet with fresh raspberries,
strawberries or blueberries for a fruit dazzler!*

WINTER AMBROSIA
"A wonderful variation of an ever-popular fruit dessert!"

3 bananas, sliced
3 oranges, peeled and diced
1/2 pound seedless grapes, red or green
1/2 cup chopped dates

2–3 tablespoons fresh lemon juice
1/4 cup freshly grated or packaged
   coconut
1 cup light sour cream

Combine fruit in a bowl; pour lemon juice over and toss gently. Chill. When ready to serve, add coconut and sour cream. Serves 6.

"Serve as a salad or dessert!"

Nutritional Analysis Per Serving

Calories: 224	Protein: 3 g	Saturated Fat: 2.9 g
Cholesterol: 11 mg	Carbohydrate: 44 g	Polyunsaturated Fat: 2.8 g
Sodium: 39 mg	Total Fat: 5.9 g	Monounsaturated Fat: 0.2 g

% of calories from fat = 22%
Diabetic Exchanges: 3 fruits, 1 fat

APPLE NUT PIE
"No crust to make!"

no-stick cooking spray
egg substitute equivalent to 1 egg
3/4 cup sugar
1/2 cup flour (use right out of the bag)
2 teaspoons baking powder
1 teaspoon vanilla
1/2 cup chopped pecans

1 1/2 cups peeled and thinly sliced
  cooking apples
1/4 teaspoon cinnamon
scant 1/8 teaspoon nutmeg
TOPPING:
vanilla non-fat frozen yogurt

Preheat oven to 350. Spray a 9-inch glass pie plate with no-stick spray. Combine egg substitute and sugar; stir in next 5 ingredients. Spoon into pie plate; top with cinnamon and nutmeg. Bake for 30 minutes. Serve warm with non-fat frozen vanilla yogurt. Serves 8.

Note: Combine all ingredients with a large spoon; do not use a mixer. If yogurt is not used for a topping, sprinkle lightly with confectioners sugar.

"Incredibly quick, delicious and easy!"

Nutritional Analysis Per Serving without Yogurt (with 1/2 Cup Yogurt)

Calories: 177 (276)	Protein: 2 (5) g	Saturated Fat: 0.5 (0.5) g
Cholesterol: 0 (0)	Carbohydrate: 33 (53) g	Polyunsaturated Fat: 1.5 (1.5) g
Sodium: 99 (99) mg	Total Fat: 5.0 (5.0) g	Monounsaturated Fat: 3.0 (3.0) g

% of calories from fat = 26 (16) %
(Not appropriate for diabetic diet)

APPLESAUCE CAKE
"Moist and spicy!"

no-stick cooking spray
1 3/4 cups sifted cake flour
1/2 teaspoon baking soda
1 teaspoon cinnamon
1/2 teaspoon allspice
1/8 teaspoon cloves
1/4 teaspoon salt
1/4 cup tub margarine

3/4 cup sugar
egg substitute equivalent to 1 egg
1 cup unsweetened applesauce
1/2 cup seedless raisins
TOPPING:
1 tablespoon sugar
1/8 teaspoon cinnamon

Preheat oven to 325. Spray a 7×11 glass baking dish with cooking spray. Sift together flour and next 5 ingredients; set aside. Cream margarine until light and fluffy; gradually beat in sugar. Add egg substitute and beat until light and fluffy; alternately add sifted ingredients and applesauce, stirring only enough to blend. Fold in raisins. Spoon batter into dish and bake 30 minutes or until center springs back when pressed gently. Cut into 24 squares (1 3/4×1 3/4 inches). Top each square with a sprinkling of cinnamon sugar. Yields 24 squares.

CINNAMON SUGAR: Mix sugar and cinnamon until well blended.

"Delicious with lemon low-fat frozen yogurt!"

Nutritional Analysis Per Square with Topping (without Yogurt)

Calories: 86	Protein: 1 g	Saturated Fat: 0.3 g
Cholesterol: 0 mg	Carbohydrate: 17 g	Polyunsaturated Fat: 0.9 g
Sodium: 68 mg	Total Fat: 2.0 g	Monounsaturated Fat: 0.8 g

% of calories from fat = 21%
Diabetic Exchange (for occasional use): 1 bread

HEALTHY HEART

ROSY APPLE COBBLER
"Flavored with cranberry cocktail!"

8 cups pared and sliced Granny Smith
  apples (approximately 8 apples)
1 1/2 cups sugar, divided
1/3 cup flour
1/2 teaspoon nutmeg

2 cups cranberry juice cocktail
1 cup Bisquick
1/3 cup milk
1 teaspoon grated lemon rind
foil, to cover dish

Preheat oven to 400. Place apples in a 9×13 glass dish. In a small bowl combine
1 1/4 cups sugar, flour and nutmeg; stir in cranberry juice until smooth. Pour mixture
over apples. Cover with foil, place on foil-covered baking sheet and bake for 30
minutes or until apples are tender. Combine Bisquick, 2 tablespoons sugar and milk
in bowl; stir until moistened. Use tablespoon to drop mixture onto hot apples to form
12 mounds. Mix remaining 2 tablespoons sugar and lemon rind; sprinkle over dough.
Bake uncovered for 20 minutes or until cobbler is golden. Serve warm. Serves 12.

"You'll be making this dish again and again!"

Nutritional Analysis Per Serving

Calories: 207	Protein: 1 g	Saturated Fat: 0.9 g
Cholesterol: 1 mg	Carbohydrate: 49 g	Polyunsaturated Fat: 0.7 g
Sodium: 121 mg	Total Fat: 1.9 g	Monounsaturated Fat: 0.3 g

% of calories from fat = 8%
(Not appropriate for diabetic diet)

OLD-FASHIONED PEACH CRISP
"Uses fresh or canned peaches!"

no-stick cooking spray
6 cups fresh peaches, peeled and sliced
  or
2 16-ounce cans sliced peaches (see
  note)
1/3 cup light corn syrup
1 teaspoon lemon juice
1 teaspoon cinnamon
1/4 teaspoon nutmeg
CRISP TOPPING:
1/3 cup sugar

5 tablespoons tub margarine
1/2 cup flour
3 tablespoons old-fashioned Quaker
  Oats
1/4 teaspoon cinnamon
1/8 teaspoon nutmeg
1/8 teaspoon salt
GARNISH:
vanilla frozen yogurt
  or
confectioners sugar

Preheat oven to 375. Spray a 9-inch glass baking dish. Place half the peaches in
dish; top with corn syrup. Add remaining peaches and next 3 ingredients. Combine
topping ingredients; blend well and press firmly over peaches. Bake 45–50 minutes.
Do not overcook. Serves 9.

TO SERVE: Top each serving with yogurt or a sprinkling of confectioners sugar.

*NOTE: Use canned peaches in either heavy or light syrup. Rinse peaches in water
and dry on toweling before using in recipe.*

"Good all year 'round!"

Nutritional Analysis Per Serving without Garnish

Calories: 199	Protein: 2 g	Saturated Fat: 1.2 g
Cholesterol: 0 mg	Carbohydrate: 35 g	Polyunsaturated Fat: 3.2 g
Sodium: 121 mg	Total Fat: 6.7 g	Monounsaturated Fat: 2.3 g

% of calories from fat = 29%
(Not appropriate for diabetic diet)

DESSERTS

CHOCOLATE SWIRL ANGEL CAKE
"Starts with a mix!"

CAKE:
1 14.5-ounce box angel food cake
  mix
1 1/3 cups water

CHOCOLATE SWIRL:
1/4 cup cocoa
1/3 cup warm water
2 tablespoons sugar

Preheat oven as directed on box. Prepare cake batter by directions on box using the 1 1/3 cups water. After flour packet is mixed in, use rubber spatula to gently fold in chocolate swirl mixture. Do not blend completely; leave swirls of chocolate in the batter. Bake as directed on box. Yields 16 slices.
CHOCOLATE SWIRL: Blend all ingredients until completely smooth.

"Serve with fresh raspberries or strawberries and a sprinkling of powdered sugar!"

Nutritional Analysis Per Serving without Fruit

Calories: 117	Protein: 4 g	Saturated Fat: 0
Cholesterol: 0	Carbohydrate: 26 g	Polyunsaturated Fat: 0
Sodium: 106 mg	Total Fat: 0	Monounsaturated Fat: 0

Diabetic Exchange (for occasional use): 1 1/2 breads

CHOCOLATE AND FRESH FRUIT

Chocolate and fresh fruit are natural partners. Try one of the two chocolate desserts on this page with Fresh Melon Balls with Lime Sauce (page 8).

DEVIL'S FOOD CUPCAKES
"Serve plain or sprinkle with powdered sugar!"

1 cup sugar
1/2 cup margarine, softened
1 egg
1 teaspoon vanilla
1 1/3 cups flour
1/2 cup cocoa

1 teaspoon baking soda
1/2 teaspoon salt
1/2 cup buttermilk or sour milk
1/2 cup boiling water
36 miniature cupcake liners
confectioners sugar (optional)

Preheat oven to 375. Cream sugar and margarine; add egg and vanilla. Mix all dry ingredients in a bowl; stir well. Alternately add dry ingredients and buttermilk to creamed mixture. Mix well after each addition. Slowly stir in boiling water; blend well. Fill paper-lined muffin cups 2/3 full. Bake approximately 13–14 minutes or until the center springs back when pressed gently. When cool, sprinkle with confectioners sugar, if desired. Yields 36 miniature cupcakes.

Note: Can be frozen.

"Moist and rich!"

Nutritional Analysis Per Plain Mini-Cake

Calories: 67	Protein: 1 g	Saturated Fat: 0.6 g
Cholesterol: 0 mg	Carbohydrate: 10 g	Polyunsaturated Fat: 1.2 g
Sodium: 91 mg	Total Fat: 2.8 g	Monounsaturated Fat: 1.0 g

Note: A portion of food containing 3 grams or less of fat is considered a low-fat serving.
Diabetic Exchange (for occasional use): 1/2 bread, 1/2 fat

HEALTHY HEART

CHOCOLATE CLOUDS
"A light, chewy cookie!"

4–5 tablespoons cocoa
1/4 cup canola oil
2 egg whites, at room temperature
1/8 teaspoon salt
3/4 cup sugar

1/2 teaspoon vanilla
1/2 teaspoon white vinegar
1/4 cup chopped pecans
no-stick cooking spray

Preheat oven to 350. Combine cocoa and oil; mix and set aside. Place egg whites in a small, deep-sided bowl; beat egg whites and salt with electric mixer until foamy. Gradually add sugar, 1 tablespoon at a time, beating well after each addition. Continue beating until stiff peaks form; beat in vanilla and vinegar. Fold in chocolate mixture and pecans. Drop batter by rounded teaspoons onto sprayed cookie sheets. Bake 10 minutes; remove from cookie sheets immediately. Yields 36 cookies.

Note: Delicious to serve with a medley of fresh fruits or sherbet.

"Tastes totally illegal!"

Nutritional Analysis Per Cookie

Calories: 37	Protein: 0	Saturated Fat: 0.3 g
Cholesterol: 0	Carbohydrate: 5 g	Polyunsaturated Fat: 0.5 g
Sodium: 10 mg	Total Fat: 2.1 g	Monounsaturated Fat: 1.3 g

Note: A portion of food containing 3 grams or less of fat is considered a low-fat serving.
Diabetic Exchange (for occasional use): 1/2 fruit, 1/2 fat

PUMPKIN COOKIES
"An extra-easy, spicy fall treat!"

no-stick cooking spray
2/3 cup tub margarine
1 cup sugar
1 16-ounce can cooked pumpkin
1 egg
2 teaspoons apple pie spice
1 1/2 teaspoons baking powder
1/2 teaspoon baking soda

1/2 teaspoon lemon extract
1 teaspoon vanilla extract
2 cups flour
ICING:
2 cups confectioners sugar
rind of one orange, grated
1/4 cup fresh orange juice

Preheat oven to 375 degrees. Spray cookie sheets and set aside. Use a mixer to blend first 9 ingredients; add flour and mix thoroughly. Drop by teaspoons onto cookie sheets. Bake for 10 minutes or until golden. Yields 60 cookies.

ICING: Blend icing ingredients; spread on cooled cookies. Icing firms as it cools.

Note: Apple pie spice is found in the spice department.

"A delicious, cake-like cookie!"

Nutritional Analysis Per Cookie

Calories: 63	Protein: 1 g	Saturated Fat: 0.4 g
Cholesterol: 5 mg	Carbohydrate: 11 g	Polyunsaturated Fat: 1.0 g
Sodium: 44 mg	Total Fat: 2.2 g	Monounsaturated Fat: 0.8 g

Note: A portion of food containing 3 grams or less of fat is considered a low-fat serving.
Diabetic Exchange (for occasional use): omit icing and count as 1/2 bread, 1/2 fat

 HEALTHY HEART NUT SUBSTITUTE
Substitute Grape Nuts for the nuts in your cookie recipes. The crunch is wonderful!

DESSERTS

SUNDAES!
"Don't you just love them?"

Start with your favorite low-fat or non-fat frozen
yogurt and use any of these delicious toppings!

HOT FUDGE

2 1/2–3 tablespoons cocoa
1/2 cup sugar
1/3 cup 1% low-fat milk

1 tablespoon canola oil
1 teaspoon vanilla

Combine all ingredients in a small saucepan; mix well and cook over low heat. Cook,
uncovered until mixture reaches a boil; reduce heat and cook for 5–7 minutes or until
mixture begins to thicken. Yields approximately 1 cup. Spoon 1 tablespoon of hot
fudge sauce over vanilla, strawberry, coffee or peppermint frozen yogurt.

HOT FUDGE WITH TOASTED ALMONDS

Top the Hot Fudge Sundae with 1 teaspoon toasted sliced almonds.

BANANA-STRAWBERRY

1 10-ounce package frozen sliced
   strawberries in syrup, thawed

2 ripe bananas, peeled and sliced

Combine partially drained, strawberries and bananas; spoon over vanilla or
strawberry frozen yogurt. Topping will make 8 sundaes.

*Note: Fresh strawberries with sugar substitute can be used in place of frozen
sweetened berries.*

PEACH MELBA

3 fresh peaches, peeled and sliced   1/2 cup raspberry or Melba sauce

Combine peaches and raspberry or Melba sauce and spoon over vanilla or peach
frozen yogurt. Topping will make 8 sundaes.

BANANA SPLIT

1 ripe banana
1 tablespoon frozen sliced
   strawberries in syrup, thawed

1 tablespoon crushed pineapple
1 tablespoon hot fudge sauce (see
   above)

Place sliced banana in the bottom of a banana split dish or bowl; top with a 4-ounce
scoop of 3 different flavors of frozen yogurt. Spoon topping over each scoop. Serves 3.

"Indulge and never feel guilty!"

Nutritional Analysis Per Serving Made with 4 Ounces Non-Fat Frozen Vanilla Yogurt and Amount of Topping Specified in Recipe						
	Calories:	Cholesterol:	Sodium:	Fat:	Fat %:	Diabetic Exchanges:
Hot Fudge	146	0	3 mg	2.0 g	13%	not appropriate
Hot Fudge with Almonds	159	0	3 mg	3.3 g	18%	not appropriate
Banana-Strawberry	170	0	1 mg	1.2 g	6%	*
Peach Melba	137	0	1 mg	1.0 g	7%	**
Banana Split	163	0	1 mg	1.5 g	9%	not appropriate

* **For occasional use only; use unsweetened frozen strawberries:** 2 fruits, 1/2 skim milk
****For occasional use only; use fresh or unsweetened frozen raspberries:** 1 1/2 fruits, 1/2 skim milk

=**LIMITING FAT IN YOUR DAILY DIET**=

Words Worth Eating suggests . . .

that you plan your daily menu ahead of time with a goal of limiting your total intake of fat to no more than 30%* of your total daily calories.

If you are having an entrée, dessert or other dish that contains more than 30% total fat, fix other dishes that are extra low in fat. The goal is to balance your intake of fat, not to eliminate fat entirely.

*Unless prescribed otherwise by your doctor

Helpful Information . . .

Cholesterol is found in all animal products (meat, fish, poultry, dairy products) but is especially high in egg yolks and organ meats. Shellfish is much lower in cholesterol than originally thought and can be included in a heart-healthy diet. Limit intake of cholesterol to less than 300 mg per day.

Saturated fats tend to raise the level of cholesterol in the blood and are therefore restricted in these recipes. These are fats that harden at room temperature and are found in most animal products and hydrogenated vegetable products.

- Saturated animal fats are meat fats from beef, lamb, pork and ham and the fat in butter, cream, whole milk and cheeses made from cream and whole milk.
- Saturated vegetable fats are found in many solid and hydrogenated shortenings and in coconut oil, cocoa butter and palm oil (used in commercially prepared cookies, pie fillings and non-dairy milk and cream substitutes).

Polyunsaturated oils are usually liquid oils of vegetable origin such as corn, cottonseed, soybean, sunflower and safflower oils. They tend to lower the level of cholesterol in the blood. Use margarine made with polyunsaturated oil and with liquid oil as the first ingredient on the label.

Monounsaturated oils are olive, canola and peanut oil. Recent studies show they may also lower blood cholesterol provided the diet is very low in saturated fatty acids.

The body can use all three types of fats, but the average person should limit fat intake to less than 30% of total calories. Of that amount, less than 10% of the total calories should come from saturated fatty acids, and no more than 10% of the total calories should come from polyunsaturated fatty acids to enhance the cholesterol-lowering process. The remainder of dietary fat should be derived from monounsaturated sources.

Note: Information is based on the National Cholesterol Education Program Recommendations, which is coordinated by the National Heart, Lung and Blood Institute; and the *American Heart Association Cookbook, 5th Edition,* 1991.

To assist you in following a low-fat diet, all recipes in
this cookbook meet the following criteria:
• 30% or less of total calories from fat
or
• 3 grams or less of fat per serving
The goal for a low-fat diet is to balance fat intake over
the entire day, rather than for each meal or food item.
